The Complete Guide to

Online
Stock Market
Investing

The Complete Guide to

Online Stock Market Investing

The Definitive 20-Day Guide

Alexander Davidson

KOGAN
PAGE

London and Philadelphia

Publisher's note

Every possible effort has been made to ensure that the information contained in this book is accurate at the time of going to press, and the publishers and author cannot accept responsibility for any errors or omissions, however caused. No responsibility for loss or damage occasioned to any person acting, or refraining from action, as a result of the material in this publication can be accepted by the editor, the publisher or of the author.

First published in Great Britain and the United States in 2002 by Kogan Page Limited as *Everyone's Guide to Online Stock Market Investing*
Second edition published in 2007 as *The Complete Guide to Online Stock Market Investing*
Reprinted 2007

120 Pentonville Road   525 South 4th Street, #241
London N1 9JN   Philadelphia PA 19147
United Kingdom   USA
www.kogan-page.co.uk

© Alexander Davidson, 2002, 2007

The right of Alexander Davidson to be identified as the author of this work has been asserted by him in accordance with the Copyright, Designs and Patents Act 1988.

ISBN-10   0 7494 4747 8
ISBN-13   978 0 7494 4747 2

British Library Cataloguing-in-Publication Data

A CIP record for this book is available from the British Library.

Library of Congress Cataloging-in-Publication Data

Davidson, Alexander, 1957-
  The complete guide to online stock market investing / Alexander Davidson. – 2nd ed.
    p. cm.
  Includes index.
  Rev. ed. of: Everyone's guide to online investing. 2002.
  ISBN-13: 978-0-7494-4747-2
  ISBN-10: 0-7494-4747-8
  1. Electronic trading of securities. 2. Investments–Computer network resources. I. Davidson, Alexander, 1957– Everyone's guide to online investing. II. Title.
  HG4515.95.D38 2006
  332.63'2202854678--dc22
                            2006030579

Typeset by JS Typesetting Ltd, Porthcawl, Mid Glamorgan
Printed and bound in Great Britain by Cambridge University Press

The ✸ factor

N✸ *capital gains tax*

N✸ *stamp duty*

N✸ *commission*

N✸ *brainer!*

There are many advantages to spread betting with Cantor Index
to find out more visit our web site or call the number below.
We allow both deposit & credit accounts.

020 7894 8050
cantorindex.co.uk

Part of the Cantor Fitzgerald Group, est. 1945

Contents

Acknowledgements   *xx*

Introduction   1

Part 1: The Basics   3

Day 1   The stock market online   5
           Overview   5
           The development of online trading   5
           The way forward   10
           Dynamic rules   11

Day 2   Initial web forays   14
           Overview   14
           Four useful sites   14
           Other useful sites   20
           The way forward   20
           Dynamic rules   20

Day 3   How to choose an online broker   21
           Overview   21
           Your choice of stockbroker   21
           Online broking   24
           The way forward   32
           Dynamic rules   33

All the research, flexibility and expertise.

(Without the expensive price tag)

Style: MARKETMASTER®

Collection: ONLINE

Colour: CYAN

Price:

£7.50

BARCLAYS
Stockbrokers

Whatever you're buying or selling, you obviously want the best deal.

And the best deal in trading is Barclays Stockbrokers, where online trades cost as little as £7.50* each.

There's more. You can also access our vast resource of stock price movements, market information, sector analysis and past performances as well as projected earnings.

So when you're looking for the best deal, we're just the ticket.

Please remember that share trading is not for everyone, when dealing in shares you can lose money as well as gain.

To find out more visit
www.stockbrokers.barclays.co.uk

BARCLAYS
Stockbrokers

Day 4   The mechanics of dealing online   **36**
   Overview   36
   First steps   36
   Trading systems   37
   The way forward   40
   Dynamic rules   40

Day 5   The streetwise online shareholder   **41**
   Overview   41
   Holding your shares   41
   Tax considerations   44
   Diversification   45
   Investment clubs   48
   Regulation and complaints   48
   The way forward   50
   Dynamic rules   50

Part 2:   Ratio Analysis and Stock Selection   **53**

Day 6   How the financial statements work   **57**
   Overview   57
   Today's accounting environment   57
   Annual report and accounts   57
   The way forward   62
   Dynamic rules   62

Day 7   Ratio analysis and macro-economic indicators   **63**
   Overview   63
   Become your own analyst   63
   Ratios   65
   Discounted cash flow analysis   69
   Macro-economic events   71
   Fundamental data resources   73
   The way forward   73
   Dynamic rules   74

Day 8   Charts galore   **76**
   Overview   76
   The theory of technical analysis   76
   Different kinds of chart   78
   The way forward   83
   Dynamic rules   83

ADVANTAGE
IS EVERYTHING

Our tight spreads give you a powerful advantage.

When trading the financial markets – advantage is everything. That's why thousands of customers Spread Bet with CMC Markets.

We offer famously tight spreads in thousands of global markets and each trade is executed across one of the fastest, most reliable trading platforms in the world. Our award-winning software also provides you with free professional charting, news and analysis and some of the most competitive margin rates available anywhere.

And if that's not advantage enough, Financial Spread Betting is completely tax free* and you can potentially profit from both rising and falling markets.

If you're trading to win, contact CMC Markets today.

Before you take advantage of our service remember Spread Betting is a leveraged product and carries a high level of risk to your capital. It is possible for you to incur losses in excess of your initial stake. Spread Betting may not be suitable for all investors, therefore ensure you fully understand the risks involved and seek independent advice if necessary.
*Tax laws can change.

Visit www.cmcmarkets.co.uk or call 0800 0933 633

Sales hours 08:00 – 19:00 (Mon-Fri) 09:00 – 17:00 (Sat-Sun)

Day 9 How technical analysis can make you money   84
Overview   84
How to use the charts   84
Chart patterns   88
Advanced theories   96
The way forward   97
Dynamic rules   97

Day 10 Secrets of technical indicators   98
Overview   98
Technical indicators   98
Charting facilities, tips and training   105
The way forward   105
Dynamic rules   106

Part 3: Specialist Investments   107

Day 11 How to win in the penny share casino   109
Overview   109
A penny for your thoughts   109
Markets   110
Types of penny share   112
Stock selection   115
Buying and selling techniques   115
Tax advantages   116
The way forward   117
Dynamic rules   117

Day 12 Pooled investment made easy   118
Overview   118
Investment funds – the lazy person's way   118
Investment trusts   121
Exchange-traded funds   122
Your pension   122
The way forward   122
Dynamic rules   123

Day 13 How to make a killing on new issues   124
Overview   124
How a new issue works   124
Research before committing your cash   127

KINGJAMES/11347

When it comes to CFDs, most companies don't know their ABCs.

At Global Trader, CFDs are our business. So while many financial institutions are now dabbling in CFDs, at Global Trader, we dabble in little else. The key to our success? Our unique combination of technological innovation, transparency and client service. If you want leveraged access to invest, long or short, in local and international markets, then talk to the people that set the standard. Get more information at **www.gt247.com** or phone us at +44 (0)20 7420 1236. See how different a CFD company can be.

<GLOBAL TRADER>
WELCOME TO THE NEW WORLD

CFDs carry a high level of risk to your capital. Only speculate with money you can afford to lose as you may lose more than your original deposit. CFDs can be very volatile and prices may move rapidly against you. Resulting losses may require further payments to be made. CFDs may not be suitable for all customers, so ensure you fully understand the risks involved and seek independent advice if necessary. Global Trader Europe Ltd is authorised and regulated by the Financial Services Authority.

How to apply successfully for new issues   128
Upon issue   129
The way forward   130
Dynamic rules   130

Part 4: Trading and Derivatives   **133**

Day 14 How to win as a share trader   **135**
Overview   135
Preparing to trade   135
Position yourself in the market   136
General trading principles   137
Money management   139
Screen-based news and data   143
The way forward   144
Dynamic rules   144

Day 15 How to profit from options and covered warrants **145**
Overview   145
How options work   145
Basic strategies   148
Advanced strategies   149
Risk warnings   150
Become your own options analyst   151
Covered warrants   153
The way forward   154
Dynamic rules   154

**Day 16 The daredevil trader: financial futures and spread
betting**   **156**
Overview   156
Financial futures   156
Spread betting   157
The way forward   170
Dynamic rules   171

**Day 17 The canny margin trader: contracts for difference and
foreign exchange**   **172**
Overview   172
Contracts for difference   172
Foreign exchange   176

Trade for
£12.50*

*Online or over the phone.

Our pricing is straightforward. Whatever the size of your transaction or the investment, you'll always pay the same dealing fee.

Combined with no annual account fee on Dealing and SIPP Dealing accounts and a single flat annual fee of £25 covering both self-select ISAs and PEPs, you can be sure of value for money when you choose Selftrade.

Visit www.selftrade.co.uk
or call 0845 0700 720

UK and international equities, ETFs, unit trusts/OEICs,
gilts, corporate bonds, covered warrants,
Listed CFDs and structured products.

selftrade

The way forward	178
Dynamic rules	178
Part 5: The Broader Picture	**179**
Day 18 Media and publicity power	**181**
Overview	181
The hidden hand of public relations	181
The press	182
The company perspective	182
Tip sheets	183
Training and seminars	186
The way forward	187
Dynamic rules	188
Day 19 Sharp operators at work	**189**
Overview	189
Unauthorized firms	189
Authorized firms	192
Access to client lists	194
Regulatory warnings and legislation	195
The way forward	195
Dynamic rules	195
Day 20 Rich dividends from reading	**197**
Overview	197
The online advantage	197
Recommended books	198
The way forward	210
Dynamic rules	210
A final word	**211**
Appendix	**213**
Useful websites	213
Complaints	218
Index	*230*
Index of advertisers	*234*

ODL Securities Limited

Since 1994 we have built up a loyal and growing base of customers who use ODL Securities to meet their 24 hour trading requirements. Our customers include retail customers, institutions & fund managers, introducing agents and brokers. We now have over 17,000 client accounts and our client assets under management have grown to over $10 billion.

Our products range from on-exchange equities, derivatives, commodities and fixed income to OTC (over the counter) spot and forward foreign exchange & precious metals, CFDs and energy derivatives. We also offer ISAs, PEPs and self invested personal pension (SIPP) products offering the full range of permitted investments. Interest is paid on all cash balances not used for margin purposes.

The ODL Corporate Finance department specialises in the resource and mining sectors. Its principal activities are raising funds in the initial stages of financing through private placements and the IPO market.

Further new product teams and senior management appointments were made in 2005 and early 2006 to further enhance the service we offer to our clients.

Equities & Options

Our customers are able to trade UK, US, Irish, continental European, Canadian and Australian exchanges.

We offer online and telephone trading in an execution-only and advisory capacity. Customers are able to trade multiple products on multiple markets, in single or multiple currencies on one trading platform. Options are used in isolation or in conjunction with equity portfolios and personal pensions for hedging purposes, enhancing returns as part of a longer term strategy, capital growth and short term speculation.

As well as access to our experienced professionals for support, customers receive regular free research and free access to live exchange data. Our advisory service offers fundamental and technical analysis and options strategy modelling. The 'Snaffler' software calculates all the options straddles and strangles that could be traded and produces a list from which we can cherry pick the best returns. The Snaffler is exclusive to ODL Securities.

Futures & Options on Futures

Since 1994 we have offered an extensive exchange-traded derivatives service. The ODL J-Trader offers the market-leading trading application for direct access to all major floor-based and electronic exchanges.

CFDs

We offer telephone and online direct market access trading on UK, continental European, Scandinavian, and US equity and index products. We do not quote fixed minimum spreads and commissions and financing charges are low. Our customers are now able to trade CFDs within a SIPP wrapper.

Spot and Forward Foreign Exchange & Precious Metals

Customers can trade on line or by phone in over 50 currency pairs and we will quote on any traded exotic currency pair. You can trade using mini or standard trading platforms and assistance is provided by experienced FX professionals via telephone or live chat.

We are now ranked as one of the largest UK non-bank participants in the foreign exchange market. Due to this level of overall order flow, we are able to offer competitive, tight spreads. Margin requirements start at one percent and we do not charge commissions or fees.

Fixed Income

Customers have access to the international fixed income bond market through our dedicated and experienced team. We provide prices and investment solutions to customers in government and corporate bonds from AAA to high yield and emerging market debt in $, € and £. You can deal in both liquid and illiquid issues efficiently to your best advantage.

Energy Derivatives

Our Energy Division provides a full execution-only, advisory and post-trade service on all crude oil and crude product instruments for retail and institutional customers. This service is available for both novice and experienced investors and the team regularly makes recommendations on option strategies covering all risk profiles.

We provide access to ICE Brent Crude and Gas Oil Exchange Options, NYMEX WTI Crude, Heating Oil and Gasoline Exchange Options during and outside exchange hours.

Spread Betting

We offer spread betting in all major financial markets. This includes UK, US, continental European, Canadian and Australian equities and indices, foreign exchange, precious metals, energy and soft commodities.

Regional Representation:
- Europe
- North America
- Middle East
- Far East
- Oceania

Regional Offices:
Head Office – London
US Office – Chicago
Japanese Office – Tokyo

www.odls.com

Regulation

ODL Securities Limited is authorised and regulated by the Financial Services Authority. Member of the London Stock Exchange. Member of Euronext.LIFFE. Designated Broker of Euronext.LIFFE.

ODL Securities Inc. operates out of the U.S and offers spot foreign exchange and futures trading. ODL Securities Inc. is registered with the Commodity and Futures Trading Commission and is a member of the National Futures Association.

ODL Securities Limited (Japan) is regulated by the Financial Services Agency.

Barclays Stockbrokers

A share dealing service that's about more than just equities

Barclays Stockbrokers is the largest execution-only stockbroker in the UK. Our award winning service will allow you to manage your investment portfolio across a variety of asset classes and make the most of all market conditions.

You can take advantage of our full range of services online, or if you want to speak to our dealing team you can do so directly over the phone. And if you prefer to hold certificates we can provide our service over the phone or by post.

Our products and services

We offer a selection of accounts so you can hold your investments any way that suits you. The range includes tax efficient wrappers such as ISAs, PEPs, and Self Invested Personal Pensions (SIPPs).

The value of all these investments and the income from them can fall as well as rise. If you are in doubt about their suitability for you, you should seek advice.

Here are just some of the products we offer:

- Equities – Trade in listed shares with the Barclays Stockbrokers Price Improver® and we'll use our existing relationships with the market makers to try and secure a better price than that quoted by the LSE (we succeed in 90% of cases).

- Investment Notes – Enjoy the combined benefits of capital protection at maturity and high growth potential with the flexibility of daily trading. Though if you sell early you may lose money.

- Funds Supermarket – Choose from over 400 funds, from 23 funds managers, at discounted initial charges, with the additional benefit of seeing all your investments in one place.

- Contracts for Difference (CFD)* – Benefit from movements in the prices of individual shares, indices, commodities or currencies without owning the underlying investment. These are not suitable for everyone. You can lose as well as gain money, in some cases more than your initial deposit.

- iShares (a type of Exchange Traded Funds) – The diversification offered by funds based investments with the flexibility of equities.

- Covered Warrants – Similar to options, you'll be able to speculate on price movements in shares, indices or commodities. These are not suitable for everyone. You can lose as well as gain money.

- Gilts – Diversify your portfolio with UK government bonds.

* Service provided by CityIndex Limited which trades as 'Barclays Stockbrokers CFDs'.

Competitive charges

We pride ourselves on offering high quality services at competitive prices. Trading via the Internet active investors will pay as little £7.50. For full details of our charges simply visit our website or call our contact centre.

Secure online trading

Your security is of paramount importance to us. As part of a leading financial institution you can rely on rigorous attention to the integrity of our technology. Our service is available for trading over 95% of the time, and in the unlikely event that you encounter any problems you can call our contact centre.

Next steps

For further information on our range of self direct investment services please visit **www.stockbrokers.barclays.co.uk** or call us on **0845 601 7788**.

Acknowledgements

The world of online stock market investing has changed so much in recent years that to prepare this second edition has been almost like writing a new book. I could not have managed it without significant help from the industry.

I would like to thank Ian Hallsworth, publisher at Kogan Page, for commissioning and encouraging this second bite of the cherry and Jon Finch who commissioned the original edition that had proved so successful. Sharescope kindly provided the charts, and Compeer provided useful research data.

My thanks are due to Gavin Oldham, chief executive at the Share Centre, David Rawlings, head of commercial development at Hargreaves Lansdown, and Rupert Dickinson, director at Barclays Stockbrokers, who were willing to discuss their line of business with me in detail.

Spread betting is a business that has new features and is developing fast, and I would like to thank Jayne Banks, marketing manager at CMC Markets, for some valuable perspectives. She also helped on contracts for difference and foreign exchange.

Some online websites were also particularly generous with their time. I would like to thank Russell Clarke, head of marketing at Hemscott plc, Francesco de Franco, who runs media relations at ADVFN, and Stuart Watson, who oversees editorial at the UK Motley Fool, for helpful discussions. Richard Beddard, editor at Interactive Investor, helped with details relating to his site.

I would like to thank the Securities & Investment Institute for giving me a front-row seat at a mid-2006 master class to the industry by Anthony Bolton, the fund manager at Fidelity Special Situations. I have reproduced some of his comments in this book.

I am grateful to my wife Aigulia and my daughter Acelia for their constant support. Some of the work on this new edition was completed in sunny Spain, where I thank Hotel Princesa in Benidorm for providing every comfort for myself and my family.

Dedication
For Aigulia with love

Risk warning

The author has made every attempt to provide up-to-date and accurate content, but the City is always developing. The investment methods described in this book have worked exceptionally well for some investors in the past, but may not suit everybody. This book is for broad educational purposes only and does not offer specific investment advice. The charts have been chosen to demonstrate technical analysis, and it is no barrier that some are a few years old.

Introduction

What this book is about

In this small book, I will show you proven ways to make money from online investing in the stock market, which you can then adapt for your own purposes. You have in your hands a course which has worked well for many over the past four years and which I encourage you to put to practical use.

To invest in shares online, if you get it right, is not just lucrative but is fun as well. You can make profits when shares are down as well as when they are up. In this book, you will find guidance for investing in all market conditions. The course is ideal for beginners, and has much to offer the more experienced investor.

Online dealing has greatly developed since the first edition of this book was published in 2002. This new edition reflects the changed environment and I have expanded the original 12 modules to 20. It is more work for you but your online investing profits could repay your efforts many times over.

The text includes a new focus on pooled investment schemes, and I have extended coverage of technical analysis and derivatives. Developments at the London Stock Exchange, including on the electronic order book and with the Alternative Investment Market, are brought up to date from latest websites and news sources.

In Chapter 2, I have taken a look for you at online stockbroking as it is today, a business no longer confined to equities. Unlike a few years ago, to trade shares online is fast, reliable and cheap.

On Day 16, I have brought spread betting up to date to include, among other extras, an explanation of rolling cash spread bets, where the spread is significantly narrower than for forward spread bets.

Become an online investor in 20 days

Time is short, and this book is designed to be read in 20 days. The information is presented in Day 1, Day 2, etc, and I suggest that you read one module a day. The modules will take you through from the basics of online investing to far beyond. You can master online investing *on top of your full-time job or other commitments*. This is important. Most people cannot just put down all their other commitments to concentrate on investing.

To make the learning process easier, the modules are broken down into succinct sections under separate headings, so that you can digest the material in bite-size chunks – on the train, in the bath, in bed, or while waiting at the bus stop. It will be helpful if you have access to the internet so that you can look up websites referred to. But even this is not essential at this stage.

The modules are to some extent interlinked, and are parts of the whole. I recommend that you do not make any new investments until you have completed all 20 modules.

Your approach

Use a highlighter pen to emphasize points that seem important, so it will be easy for you to go back to them. This book is not a precious first edition that you hardly dare touch. *You must make this material your own.*

In so doing, do not expect an easy ride. But if you put an effort into learning, by the time you have finished, you will have a sound grasp of ratio analysis, discounted cash flow analysis, reading the charts, choosing your broker, the mechanics of buying and selling shares, new issues and a whole lot more.

You will find that this book guides you towards *thinking like a successful investor*, which is far more important than cramming either investment facts or – worse still – technology. At the end of each module there is a summary of important points covered.

Time to put your books away

Once you have read this book, you should be ready to invest with confidence. Be prepared to make mistakes, and take responsibility for these. Although I am giving you all the help that I can, any investment is your own choice – and at your own risk.

That is the preliminaries over. Now hold onto your hat, dear reader, as I am going to take you on the most thrilling journey of your life, the rollercoaster ride of online stock market investing.

The author invites you to visit his website at www.flexinvest.co.uk and to contact him by e-mail through this route.

Part 1

The Basics

The stock market online

Overview

In this module, we will consider the skills you need to develop into a first-rate online investor. We will look at the advantages of investing via the internet and at some of the ups and downs that investors have experienced. I will show you how to harness the power of value investing. We will discuss how analysts work, investment clubs, and investing abroad.

The development of online trading

The formative years

Online investing has had a fast evolution. It started to become popularized in 1995 and, boy, was there progress. In the earliest days, only about one trade a day was done online. Trading was confined to UK equities at the market price, with no limit orders to enable deals within specified prices. The first customers placed orders by e-mail, which has been replaced by an automated process.

There was a standard 30-minute delay in share prices shown on screen, which put private investors at a major disadvantage to the pros. They were willing to pay to upgrade to a 15-minute delay. Today there are free *real-time* prices.

In the mid-1990s and up to a few years later, the online dealers tended to have a tiered charging structure, where the costs of a trade decreased with its size. This has largely been replaced by a flat fee structure, often with a reduction for frequent traders.

By early April 2005, there were as many as 635,000 private investors with online dealing accounts. In recent years, the range of securities traded has expanded. Some of the larger brokers now trade derivatives, foreign exchange and bonds, and offer ISAs, self-invested personal pensions (SIPPs) and investment funds.

Online share trading services have started breaking into profit. They are now more reliable and better serviced, and the facilities are better value for money. The online stockbrokers' websites have become so user-friendly that a child could put them to full use. Using the best sites, you not only can buy and sell shares, obtain real-time quotes and track your portfolio, but you also have access to analysis and financial news flow. You may apply stock selection filters.

Some online services are available via WAP (wireless application protocol) on mobile phones and handheld devices. As yet, the services are limited, but the potential is vast. You can now use the search engine Google on your mobile to access WAP content.

One downside of online stock market investing is that real human contact is often missing. If you are the type of person who needs your hand held while making your investment decisions, or needs somebody else to make them for you, you will prefer telephone or face-to-face contact. The internet is not enough, but it will still be very useful.

History repeats itself

The internet has facilitated trading, but markets behave as they always did. Investors move in herds and they buy too late and sell too early. Market movements reflect the hopes and fears of investors and are exaggerated. In late 1999 and early 2000, the bull market in the UK and continental Europe, led by the US, was at a height. Investors were rushing to buy telecommunications and high-tech stocks, which sent the share prices still higher.

The companies were priced far above value. They were sometimes months old and had no proven earnings, and maybe little in the way of revenues. At this stage, stock market analysts were valuing internet stocks on future revenues. They used innovative measures such as eyeballs – how many visits the site received, and stickability – for how long they lasted. The bank's corporate finance department would tell analysts what to write about a company that was, or it hoped would become, a corporate client.

In March 2000, the market underwent a massive correction, led by the overvalued internet stocks that had been heralded as the forerunners of a new economy.

Some investors would have made money – in some cases quite a lot of it – if they had cashed in their paper profits on high-tech stocks on the cusp of the downturn. But many missed the boat and were left holding fallen stars. It cost some traders their homes.

On the bright side, the crash taught a generation of investors the benefits of short selling, which is to sell shares you do not own in the belief they will fall in value and to buy, hopefully at a lower price, to complete the transaction. It helped to spawn a revolution in derivatives trading, where, for retail investors taking a short position is possible, particularly in spread betting (Day 16) and contracts for difference (Day 17).

Private investors are at an advantage over fund managers in that they have more flexibility to buy and sell because their holdings are smaller and they are not similarly answerable to external parties. But because they are small they are not given the same quality and timeliness of the information required to make investment choices.

To guide buying and selling decisions, investors may use technical analysis, which is to read the charts. Investment banks do not use this method much because, cynics say, fund managers avoid it, preferring fundamental analysis which they can work into their models and show they have added value, so helping to justify their jobs. Investment banks need access to fund managers not just as clients, but also to provide feedback on stockflow to assist proprietorial trading.

But, if technical analysis is the only guide, it can be dangerous. Fundamental analysis is always desirable for medium- to long-term investors because share prices move eventually in line with stock valuations, although the correlation is often temporarily out of kilter.

Markets can swing violently, taking stocks with them regardless of valuations. A major skill of investing is to make the big moves not too far ahead of inevitable major market adjustments. It is precious few stocks that are worth holding through a bear market.

The FTSE-100 is an index which represents the 100 largest UK quoted companies and is the most widely used proxy for the UK stock market. On 30 December 1999, it reached a then all-time high of 6,930. By 12 March 2003, the index had plummeted to 3,287. In the face of such volatility, many investors do nothing and lose money. They are like rabbits frozen before the headlamps of an approaching car.

When stocks are low, it is a good time to buy. By early March 2006, the index had recovered much of its loss to reach 5,900 and many users of our investment methods sold out. Their timing may not always have been perfect but it was in the ballpark. They had bought when stocks were low because they were *value* investors who, as an added bonus, had an eye on *growth*. To appreciate when to sell was trickier but they knew it was dangerous to wait until the index had topped because it could then fall fast again.

Don't rely on analysts

Successful investors consider analysts' comments but never make them the priority. Top analysts do not usually aim their recommendations at private clients and in the past at least, they have lacked independence.

The April 2003 Spitzer settlement in the United States brought some of the problems out into the open. It punished perceived issuance of biased stock recommendations and highlighted the conflict of interest between the lucrative investment banking division and the research division within the same firm.

The UK felt the reverberations, and regulatory control of analysts has tightened up. But analysts still depend on the companies that they watch to provide data and news flow. They are reluctant to issue a *sell* recommendation. Instead, they may issue a long-term *hold* or *reduce*. They may reveal true thoughts about the company only to favoured clients.

Investing techniques

The bull market of 2006 showed investors repeating old patterns. They bought because the market was high. Professionals with vested interests will hate me for saying this, but the dark side of online stockbroking is that it encourages such reckless trading. Anybody who has sufficient funds and access to the internet can open an online account, and buy and sell shares. You need simply sit and tap the right keys on your computer.

If you practise money management, you can act fast to reduce losses, but few amateurs have the skill. Like value investing, it can be taught. This book takes you a long way (see Day 14).

When to buy and sell

At its most basic, value investing involves buying undervalued stocks cheaply, and waiting until they rise substantially before selling out. Like any successful investing system, it gives the lie to the Random Walk theory, which suggests that if you select stocks at random, they will perform at least as well on average as those picked on value criteria.

As an investor in value stocks, you should also have an eye on growth and a good dose of common sense. You should first have a pension, life assurance, and rainy-day money – perhaps £5,000 stashed in the highest-interest account that you can find. You should own your own home. The stock market is not for playing with the cash that you need.

It needs courage to buy a share when it has fallen sharply in price and nobody else is buying, but this is often when you can pick up a bargain. As a value investor, you must take the long view. In assessing a company, you cannot shirk the numbers. Days 6 and 7 will give you an understanding of the basics of accounting and ratio analysis.

Consider qualitative factors. The gap between price and true value is likely to be closed faster if the underlying company has a strong franchise, and is a market leader or close to it, with growth prospects. It helps if the management is capable, and it should be, above all, honest. The broader market should not concern you because, over the medium to long term, good and bad news tend to balance out.

City professionals are more successful at stock picking than most. They are exposed to markets all day long and are savvy about investment strategy. They know to buy when the markets have hit rock-bottom and to sell before a bull market has risen too high. They select their own stocks and so are comfortable using online brokers, which normally are cheap but do not offer advice.

To decide when to sell, like most investing decisions, is an art and not a science. In April through to three weeks into June 2006, the FTSE-100 lost about 8 per cent of its value but a significant number of investors had sold out in advance. Private investors sold £3.1 billion of shares in February and March 2006 compared with only £959 million in April and May, according to research by Capita Registrars.

Market feedback suggested it was investor attitude and not market fundamentals that had driven the retreat. The bull market had seemed tired for months earlier and, with a high oil price and talk of raising interest rates, it was looking increasingly unsustainable. It had lasted more than three years, which is long by historical standards, and assets had become expensive.

Commodities and some emerging markets stocks fell up to 40 per cent in value in May and June 2006, and there was a feeling they had further to go. Some of the newly established funds were waiting for a temporary market rise which would give them a chance to sell out more profitably.

Anyone who wanted to stay invested in a slumping market could buy defensive stocks such as pharmaceuticals and, in mid-2006, media, because it was out of favour. The market recovered and, on 20 October, the FTSE-100 index reached a new five-year trading high, within a whisker of breaching the 6,200 level. Many stocks were overvalued on fundamentals and buying was sustained often on bid speculation, sometimes with a limited basis in reality. The market was showing further symptoms of a tired bull market.

Invest abroad

Consider applying your investing skills abroad, but only after you have gained some UK experience. You will need to consider the exchange rate as well as the share price. The US market is the first mover and other global markets follow. European markets tend to swing in tandem.

The internet is a key research tool. Through a search engine such as Google you can gain access to stock data, market reports and stock exchange profiles in various regions of the world.

If you have significant investing experience, consider emerging markets. The risks are high but so are the potential rewards. In Brazil, Russia, Turkey and India, share prices quadrupled between the start of 2003 and May 2006.

Jim Rogers, a legendary commodity investor, says that Russia and the ex-Soviet Union countries have terrible prospects, not least because they lack infrastructure and do not invest in themselves. He puts his faith in China.

But some who, unlike Rogers, are short-term stock traders have made a lot of money out of Russian stock market volatility in recent years.

American depositary receipts (ADRs)

Some markets outside Western Europe are so illiquid that, once you have bought shares, you cannot easily sell them. If you complained about how the deal was handled, you would as a foreign investor receive little priority. It will be almost impossible to conduct court cases from outside the country.

You can avoid these problems through buying American depositary receipts (ADRs), which are US domestic securities representing ownership of a foreign stock. General depositary receipts, or GDRs, are an equivalent that may be found in London.

ADRs work out slightly more expensive than the underlying securities, but they are liquid, and give you access to proper reporting information about the company. You will be notified of dividends and structural reorganizations, and there will be proper news coverage. To find out more, visit the ADR website of US investment bank JP Morgan at www.adr.com.

The way forward

Unless you are a pure technician, to become a successful investor, you will need the intellectual capacity to interpret figures. Fundamental investing is not for everybody but, if you are determined, you can learn the qualities, skills and self-discipline required, almost no matter what your age or circumstances.

In the next module, we will look at four websites that will help get you off to a flying start.

Dynamic rules

- Online stockbroking services are user-friendly, but human contact may be lacking.
- Share prices move in line with underlying values, but are often temporarily out of kilter.
- Do not rely on analysts' recommendations. They are normally aimed at institutional investors, who know how to read between the lines.
- Do not invest in the stock market until you have a pension, life assurance and other basics in place.
- As a value investor, you need to buy at a low price and sell high. To recognize stock bargains, it helps to understand accounting.
- Invest in a business franchise that is hard to compete against, market leadership and, ideally, experienced management.
- Put money in emerging market stocks for high rewards but high risks.

ABOUT STOCKTRADE

Stocktrade is the Execution-only division of Brewin Dolphin Securities Ltd., the largest independent portfolio manager and stockbroker in the UK.

Stocktrade has been establishing new standards in stockbroking and customer services since 1993. On 30th November 1998 Stocktrade was the first broker in the UK to offer on-line equity trading to private investors and in February 2000 it launched SpeechTrade™, the UK's first automatic voice activated stock price quoting service.

As an execution-only broker, Stocktrade does not offer investment advice but instead deals and settles transactions for investors who make their own decisions. Stocktrade provides a range of trading facilities including on-line, by telephone or by post, to both private and corporate investors in both certificated and electronic form.

Our services

At Stocktrade we believe in delivering choice and value with a personal touch. That means when you call us you speak directly to a member of our experienced dealing staff.

We operate a choice of accounts for our internet traders, they can operate a nominee account with all shares being in our nominee name or opt to retain the shares in their name by operating a Crest personal membership account. Along with the ability to place orders 'at quote' our clients can view a real time valuation of their portfolio and historical stock and cash information online. We offer a full telephone back up service for times when online access if not convenient or you require a more personalised facility. We aim to provide a pricing structure that is straight forward and has no complex hidden charges for value added services such as statements. Once an internet client exceeds 50 trades within any given time period we reduce our commission from 0.4% to 0.2% minimum £14.50. Our dealing platform is easy to use with each trade being confirmed online and also by means of a posted contract note. All of our internet accounts are ran in conjunction with an interest bearing deposit account to settle transactions.

For clients who prefer the more traditional telephone trading service we offer a range of dealing accounts depending on what they require. This includes a Nominee account, Crest account and certificated account.

If sometimes the account you require is not clear to you or you require more information about any of our accounts you can refer to our website **www.stocktrade.co.uk**. There you can access our Account finder which provides guidance on what account may suit you and also detailed information on each account type, all which may help you find a share dealing account more tailored to your requirements.

We now also have an area of our website designed specifically for Financial Intermediaries. AgentTrade has been designed to complement our well established telephone and postal service we offer Financial Intermediaries. Stocktrade's dedicated intermediaries team also look after all aspects of your account and answer any queries you may have. Our aim is to offer a dealing service that is tailored to meet your requirements, with AgentTrade we can offer you greater control and access than ever before. More detailed information appears on our website.

Brewin Dolphin

Brewin Dolphin Securities Limited ("BDS") is the principal operating company of Brewin Dolphin Holdings PLC which is listed on the London Stock Exchange. BDS is authorised and regulated by the Financial Services Authority and is a member of the London Stock Exchange.

BDS is the largest independent private client portfolio manager in the UK. The Group manages £19 billion of funds on behalf of more than 100,000 clients, and of this £8.5 billion is on a discretionary basis. BDS has 35 offices and is corporate adviser to 133 small and medium sized quoted companies.

Initial web forays

Overview

Online stock market investing is about using the internet – not just for the mechanical process of trading shares and derivatives at competitive prices, but also for data, news and analysis.

In this brief section, I shall point out some good sites that get you started as an investor.

Four useful sites

Be selective about information

Investment technology has created more of a level playing field among investors, according to Anthony Bolton, fund manager at Fidelity Special Situations. 'It is great for the private investor, but there is an information overload. What you don't look at is as important as what you do', he says.

A good general site may provide most of your research, news flow and educational needs when you are starting out. The four sites discussed in the paragraphs below serve the private investor well and any, or all, of them is a good place to start.

1. Motley Fool UK – www.fool.co.uk

Here is an idiosyncratic website which has educational value, in particular for novice investors who do not have a trading mentality. You may outgrow the Motley Fool UK website, but you will not be able to forget it. It is far from perfect but it has educated a generation of young investors and inspired them to think for themselves. The UK Fool, nine years old in September 2006, has come of age. It is a more professional product than in its early days and more sober.

In 1997, David Berger, a UK-based general practitioner (GP), was working part time to establish the UK Fool (www.fool.co.uk). The Fool was iconoclastic and persuasive although, in common with the financial services industry it criticized, not always right. The approach was heavily modelled on that of the site's US parent (www.fool.com). 'We're amateurs,' Berger told me with a shrug when we once met in the small London basement flat that served as the site's start-up HQ. He was too modest, although, in those early days, the quirky writing style was out of kilter with conventional journalism.

The Fool has tried to teach users of its site to pick their own stocks and make their own investment decisions. There has been an emphasis on understanding the underlying company, and on keeping trading costs low. The site was, and still is, run by self-styled Fools (with a large F) in the Shakespearean sense, who tell the king the truth when others merely flatter him. They are critical of the Wise, who are commission-hungry financial services salespeople, including stockbrokers, tipsters and the like.

The Fool had an enveloping culture, and it fast created almost a cult. Berger talked to me of how the approved ways of doing things were 'very Foolish', meaning to ask the right innocent questions. His vision was to expand the Fool concept beyond financial services. It turned out to be too ambitious.

Berger had brought to the table his own talents, which included a tongue-in-cheek writing style that in places reached rare levels of hilarity, and a good knowledge of the biotechnology sector. In those early days, the writing style was a little wild and it pushed the Fool culture, says Stuart Watson, who has been with the operation seven years and now runs the editorial department. 'This was necessary to establish the brand, but it became less important as the company became more mass market,' he says.

In those early days, the Motley Fool focused 80 per cent on the stock market and 20 per cent on personal finance investment, according to Watson. The site shunned technical analysis and the trading mentality, and it leaned heavily towards value, growth and high-yield investing. It urged investors to avoid actively managed unit trusts but instead to buy tracker funds, where the charges were low and the performance, after all costs, usually bent the market average. Jim Slater, the private investor guru, spoke highly of the UK Motley Fool.

The Fool produced reams of material online to educate investors. It ran online portfolios, which were not tip sheets but where the Fool bought shares, and kept a live online commentary about their performance. The Fool made a lot of mistakes in its stock selections but it was frank about its thought processes online. An online community of like-minded Fools was building up through the bulletin boards.

In 2001, a year after the high-tech stock market bubble had burst, Berger quit his job and returned to being a GP full time. The show seemed gradually to lose some of the earlier sparkle. The online portfolios eventually disappeared because, according to Watson, they took more time to keep up than the viewing statistics justified.

In the five years leading to mid-2006, the UK Motley Fool has increasingly focused more on personal finance than stock market investment. A spokesman says: 'Fewer people look at our stock market material these days but they spend longer on it than they do on the personal finance areas of our site.' The site contacts 2.3 million subscribers with e-mail letters twice a week. A smaller audience also receives a twice-weekly e-mail dedicated to investing. The site has editorial and news, commentary and one subscription tip sheet, which uses a wide range of stock-picking techniques. The style of investment advocated by the site reflects that of the writers employed at any given time and is not decided centrally, according to Watson.

The site takes revenue from selling advertising space and, more substantially, from referring its customers to financial services via its product comparison centres. The online discussion boards are not sponsored but some are dedicated to the products of specific firms such as Barclays Stockbrokers and Legal & General.

2. Interactive Investor – www.iii.co.uk

Interactive Investor has undergone some changes in ownership and since 2002, when the first edition of this book was published, the site has improved in quality, breadth and user-friendliness. It is now not to be missed, unless you have an ear very close to the market.

Interactive Investor brings you news, online message boards, and a wide variety of stock market and other financial services information, clearly set out, up to date, and mostly free. The share tips are from some of the biggest names in the field.

The site offers a low-cost stockbroking service, as well as facilities for trading contracts for difference (CFDs) and spread betting, complete with educational material and some simulated trading opportunity. For a subscription, you can obtain desktop trading systems to give you real-time streamed prices in your portfolio. For a slightly higher fee, you may have Level II data, which, as we shall see in Day 3, reveals the depth of orders in the market and the prices individual market makers are charging.

You will find here indices, the most active stocks, and a section headed *Extreme stocks* where you can find those with the tightest spreads, largest turnover, largest pre-tax profit and similar. This is all very useful for getting a feel for the market as well as for selecting your own stocks.

Interactive Investor, like many sites, provides a *winners and losers* list, which pinpoints stocks to watch. Some great stock market traders backed the thinking behind it even before online publication of such lists was possible. In early 20th-century America, great trader Jesse Livermore bought stocks at new highs on rising volume, and he sold those that had reached an all-time low.

Heat maps accessible through Interactive Investor show you individual stocks in boxes. If the background is blue, it shows the stock is up, if red, that it is down, and white means no change. You can summon a heat map for sectors. The concept demonstrates the claimed Chinese proverb that a picture is worth a thousand words.

A stock-filtering system is available to list those stocks that fit fundamental criteria that you specify. It is like having your own research assistant. There are facilities for trading contracts for difference (CFDs) and spread betting. Educational material is provided and there are simulated CFD trading facilities.

Fantasy stock portfolios are run online for educational purposes at Interactive Investor. City analyst and author Peter Temple set up growth, income, ethical and retirement portfolios in 2001 and 2002. Over the respective periods to July 2006, the funds have handsomely beaten their benchmarks.

From 2006, Interactive Investor has featured portfolios run by John Mulligan, which are growth, income and speculative. Mulligan is a former investment banker who uses a proprietary mechanical stock-picking system called STAR (Selections for growth at a reasonable price). It is based on Mulligan's discovery that, over 10 years, a broad range of shares where projected earnings are above average and current valuations are below average has outperformed the broader market.

To maintain the interest of the community, the site has now started a blog to which employees may contribute. 'Because we have such an active community, who rely on the services and information we provide, this is a way of reaching out to them, and increasing our relevance to their day-to-day trading and investing. They can participate too – everyone's free to comment,' says Richard Beddard, editor, Interactive Investor.

3. ADVFN – www.advfn.com

ADVFN is a comprehensive website for investors at every level. It was established in 1999 and was launched on the Alternative Investment Market in March 2000. It focuses on stock markets, commodities, futures and options and foreign exchange but, unlike Interactive Investor and the UK Motley Fool, it leaves aside personal finance.

You may access from the front page a large number of services and facilities. Some say it gives cluttered appearance but, according to a spokeswoman, it dispenses with some of the need to navigate. The site is constantly adding new tools.

Traders and investors use the site in roughly equal proportions, according to the spokeswoman. 'Some users of the site are day traders and others deal twice a year. We have tools for both,' she says. Many traders use ADVFN because so much is available free. Some customers may use the site to get a quick quote and others for access to a wide range of information and tools. The site has some classy columnists, including Alpesh Patel and Robbie Burns.

There is free access to real-time streaming stock prices but it is contended, meaning that if the site becomes crowded, users may be knocked off and have to refresh, according to the spokeswoman. For technical analysts there is free access to comprehensive charting facilities, and related threads are prominent on the bulletin boards.

For fundamental investors, access to financial data such as profit and loss accounts, balance sheets and key statistics is free. As a next step, Filter X, a stock-screening tool, is part of a package costing £5 a month. There is access to Level II data starting at £30 a month, and to NASDAQ TotalView, a Level II-style system for US stocks, which shows a breakdown of multiple orders.

The bulletin boards of ADVFN have 10,000–12,000 posts a day, which makes them the busiest on any financial website in the UK, according to the spokeswoman. 'There is a lot of conversation and it gets rowdy. We don't moderate because it would make us editors, which would open up a can of worms. But if someone complains about racist, sexist comments or similar we'll remove the posting,' she says. The bulletin boards for paid subscribers are sometimes more sober. Individuals may post a message accessible either only to other paying subscribers or to anybody.

One of the most popular free facilities on ADVFN is to create your own monitor page and fill it up with indices and stocks from any exchanges featured on the site. You will be able to watch and make side-by-side comparisons of price changes in real time and other data such as the high and low prices, trading volume, spread (difference between buying and selling price), and last trade.

Users of the UK site have international access. The front page has links to world exchanges, a world overview, and foreign exchange. If you go to another country's exchange, you can get access to indices, winners and losers, and quotes for any stock listed on that exchange. ADVFN has a significant number of US users and also has sites in French, Italian, Japanese and Brazilian. The sites are geo-typified and so are in the countries' own language.

4. Hemscott (www.hemscott.com)

Hemscott has evolved from Hemmington Scott, a publishing company established in 1985, which produced the Hambro Company Guide, later to become The Hemscott Company Guide, and Really Essential Financial Statistics (REFS), a compendium of financial ratios and statistics for quoted companies devised by private investor stock market guru Jim Slater.

In December 1999 Hemmington Scott separated into a publishing company, HS Financial Publishing Ltd, and Hemscott.NET Group, the data provider. Hemscott was formed and it gained Hemmington Scott's proprietary database, which at that time contained 15 years of data. HS Financial became its biggest data client. In 2000, Hemscott listed on the Alternative Investment Market (see Day 11) and, in 2001, it changed its name to Hemscott plc, a global group of which Hemscott.com is part. Hemscott plc does most of its work in a business-to-business environment, supplying raw data to stockbrokers such as TD Waterhouse, and providing white-level business solutions. It is also a leader in online investor relations.

Hemscott.com, known as Hemscott, has a consumer website and, unlike its competitors such as Digitallook (www.digitallook.com), it provides almost entirely its own data. Russell Clarke, head of marketing, says: 'We have an in-house quality assurance process. We have teams of people who spend all day going through the annual reports, news feeds, regulatory news, releases and similar. They add up figures, check them, and input the information into our data bases, and then it's checked all over again.'

Hemscott presents enough data free to enable site users interested in investing to 'be informed so that they can make their investment decisions,' according to Clarke. There are also Hemscott Premium and Hemscott Premium Plus subscription-level services, which, along with advertising, bring in revenue. The Premium Plus service offers subscribers up to eight years' data and five or six useful tools.

The site provides live share prices, lists of advisers to quoted companies, which can be hard to obtain elsewhere, and a corporate calendar, which lists, for example, when Vodafone is holding its next AGM. There are news feeds from the London Stock Exchange and AFX. The personal finance coverage is built around sponsored promotions. It includes, for example, a list of top-ten mortgage providers.

The users of Hemscott include a high proportion of high net worth individuals aged 35 to 60, according to Clarke. 'We treat our site users like a quality newspaper treats its readers. We have the highest quality material, but slip in some lighter stuff – our information exchange forums, Sudoku puzzles and a terrific wine guide.' Hemscott provides *Times Online* with its business information and *The Sunday Times* with data for its Rich List. The site has 300,000 registered users and user feedback suggests that it is clean and easy to navigate.

Other useful sites

There are other useful sites. MoneyAM (www.moneyam.com) was set up partly by a breakaway movement from ADVFN and provides a useful alternative. Committed traders should visit Trade2win (www.trade2win.com), which has perhaps the best bulletin boards for traders on the internet. Breakingviews.com (www.breakingviews.com) was set up by Hugo Dixon, a journalist who had headed up the *Financial Times* Lex column, and it provides daily comment on financial markets online to subscribers and by syndication to the *Wall Street Journal*. The service has won respect.

For stock market news and other financial news, see Citywire (www. citywire.co.uk), Reuters (www.reuters.co.uk) and Bloomberg (www.bloom berg.com). Watch the London Stock Exchange's website at www.london stockexchange.com. Keep an eye on the website of *Investors Chronicle* (www. investorschronicle.co.uk). For news and comment on financial services, visit AWD Moneyextra (www.moneyextra.com).

The way forward

In this module we have looked at four great general websites, and I have referred you to a few others. The content of the sites will make more sense once you have finished the book, but you will benefit from starting to explore them now.

Dynamic rules

■ Use the internet to obtain share prices and investment data, news and analysis. You can obtain much from one general site, which saves you having to switch.

How to choose an online broker

Overview

In this module, we will focus on how to choose your broker. We are focused mainly on online brokers, but will briefly consider the longer-established alternatives of discretionary and advisory broking services.

Your choice of stockbroker

If you buy and sell shares online, you are usually dealing with an execution-only stockbroker, which executes your trade without giving advice. This way, you will take charge of your own financial destiny – which is a wonderful thing but the onus is on *you* to make the right investment decisions.

The traditional advisory broking service operates usually as an alternative to the online for those who need their hands held, but the charges are higher for a not always very effective service, and it is losing market share. 'Old-style stockbroking is manpower intensive and it is being squeezed out. There now tends to be polarization between online broking and investment management,' says Gavin Oldham, founder and CEO at the Share Centre.

The broker or investment manager will run a discretionary portfolio for larger clients. The charges are lower than on investment funds (see Day 12) and in 2004, averaged 0.76 per cent of money under management, according to Compeer.

Don't Listen to Terry: Plan Your Investments Carefully

Increasingly, people are taking control of their finances and making investment decisions for themselves. The internet has been one of the major driving forces, empowering everyday investors with the sort of tools once the preserve of the professional. They plan for buying a new home, children's education, building a nest egg and retirement. But just how do they go about it?

There are two methods of investment planning: you can consider your needs, attitude to risk and available cash before making an informed decision. Or, far easier, you can just do what Terry says. Everyone knows Terry. He can usually be found on a Thursday night in the Hare and Hounds supping lager and enjoying a game of darts. Terry usually has a share tip or has heard about a great new investment scheme. The problem with listening to Terry is that he takes no account of the aspects of financial planning that are essential to successful investing.

There are three aspects of financial planning that you should take account of before listening to (or better still, ignoring) Terry: your personal circumstances, long-term planning and the choice of accounts you require.

Your Personal Circumstances

When Terry recommends an investment it is only because he has heard that it's going to do well. What he ignores is just how risky the instrument is and how much risk your circumstances allow you to accept. He ignores whether it will complement your other investments or even if it meets your investment needs.

When selecting investments you should consider not only your attitude to risk but also your needs. People who lose out on investments sometimes blame the financial instrument. But often there is nothing wrong with investment products themselves, only their appropriateness to investors' circumstances. For instance, if you are a higher rate taxpayer, you probably want to select an investment for growth and not income, not only do you not need income but you will be paying 40% of it away in income tax. You will probably only want to trade in volatile instruments such as covered warrants if you have the time to monitor their movements. You might only be prepared to dabble in higher risk stocks if you already hold a diversified portfolio of blue chip investments.

Long-term Planning

Investments should be planned over the long term, taking into account your investment objectives. This does not mean you can't stock pick, in fact many people are very successful at trading. But it should be in the context of a rounded investment strategy rather than buying on Terry's tip and crossing your fingers. Make sure you understand the company's activities and just what makes its price move. For this you'll need to research. Look at its price chart, read the news, examine its accounts and consider analyst consensus views. Your broker should make this data available.

Building a diversified portfolio is the surest way of planning for the long term. To do this you should invest in a range of quality investments including UK and international shares, collectives and bonds. You might also want to use specialist products such as covered warrants or CFDs which can act as leverage or indeed reduce the risk of your portfolio by hedging positions.

Choice of Accounts

Your investments should not only grow but should be tax efficient and appropriate for your needs. Terry might only talk of random hot tips but investment is about more than just the instruments. Using an ISA will make your investments more tax efficient, with profits avoiding capital gains tax. By the way, if your holdings warrant it, making use of the annual capital gains tax allowance, by taking profits, will also pay dividends over the long term.

Paying into a pension not only helps provide for your future but it is also one of the most tax efficient ways to invest since you get tax relief on all contributions. For those who like to manage their own financial affairs a Self-Invested Personal Pension (SIPP) allows you to make all investment decisions in your pension fund. Terry won't have a pension so telling him you have a SIPP will keep him at bay.

Don't be a Terry. Consider your needs, attitude to risk and plan your investment strategies carefully. And choose a broker who offers trade execution, access to shares, funds, bonds and warrants as well as ISAs and SIPPs at a price you are prepared to pay.

Stephen Barber, Product Manager, Selftrade

All views or opinions expressed are solely those of the author and do not necessarily represent those of Selftrade

If you are using an advisory or discretionary service, be selective. Traditional broker standards vary enormously. The broker will often play a game of hard to get, particularly if you would not be a large client.

Provincial brokers tend to give small clients much more time and attention than their London counterparts.

Anywhere in the country, there are far too many brokers who do not know what they are doing and will put you into unsuitable shares and lose you money. Some do it because they are focused on generating short-term commissions (see also Day 19).

Make sure that the investment strategy of any broker you deal with matches your own. If you like to invest in safe blue chips, do not use a broker who specializes in speculative small companies.

Never rely completely on your broker's tips, but do your own research as well. If you have a discretionary account, keep an eye on what the firm is doing with your money. Once the fund is completing 40–50 trades a year, this is the level at which the broker often receives commission, and it may affect his judgement.

In the past, a few brokers have attempted a business model that combines advisory with execution-only and the results have been disastrous. It works only if the two are kept separate. Some traditional advisory brokers today have distinct online divisions which are execution-only and operate like any other online broker. From the firm's perspective, if the online brokerage is managed correctly, it can provide leads for the advisory or discretionary broking service.

Online broking

Pros and cons

When you use an online broking service, you must take full responsibility for your buying and selling decisions. Nobody makes a profit on every trade but you must aim to get it right more often than not. You will need skills not just in stock selection and asset allocation but also in money management.

These skills are covered in this book and you will find them useful even if you have an advisory or discretionary broker and simply want to understand the implications of investment choices.

Online brokers have the major market share because of four distinct practical advantages:

■ *Low cost.* Some of the larger brokers in particular have made cost synergies and have a leaner, more efficient infrastructure with less manual intervention. This, coupled with high volumes of trade, helps to keep charges low.

■ *Accessibility.* You can visit your broker's website 24 hours a day and have access to your portfolio, with the latest available share prices. You may often pull up charts showing price movements of selected stocks or indices, and fundamental data. Through some firms you can place deals after trading hours, and they will be executed when the market opens the next morning.

■ A *fast dealing service.* The speed at which you can trade online compares favourably with traditional broking.

■ *Small size dealing.* This could be useful when you are starting out as an investor.

Broker check list

Once you have decided to use an online broker, you will find a vast range of firms at your disposal, with different strengths and weaknesses. You can choose from the many in the UK or from continental Europe or the United States.

For the purpose of this book, we will be looking mainly at the UK online broking industry. It starts with dealing services offered by company registrars. They are for shareholders who own shares as a result of a demutualization or privatization.

Beyond this level, the industry is polarized between firms like E*Trade, which target active traders, and those like Hargreaves Lansdown, which target the main retail space. 'As time goes on, this kind of polarization will increase,' says Rupert Dickinson, director at Barclays Stockbrokers.

In selecting your broker, you may find that, for trading purposes, big is best. As a broad generalization, the larger participants are better able to obtain the best prices and offer the keenest commissions and the most useful frills, such as research and news facilities. They may have a more solid infrastructure, which comes into its own at times when there is a rush on to buy or sell shares. A large firm should allow you to deal in shares and derivatives from the same account and, if possible, the same screen.

But whether you are a good broker is not just about being large or small, according to David Rawlings, head of commercial development at Hargreaves Lansdown. 'Larger brokers do clearly have the resources to invest in systems and achieve economies of scale but can, if not properly managed, lose quality of service,' he says.

Oldham of the Share Centre agrees. 'If a broker is a branch of a clearing bank, it could be putting an emphasis on insurance or mortgage sales to suit the parent's needs. System development could be constrained, and so could flexibility.'

There are other factors that you should consider in your choice of broker. I suggest that you put these 10 on your radar: image; range of services; dealing costs; price of trade; research and news; smooth running and security; limit orders and stop losses; trading hours; fantasy trading; and new equity issues. Let us take each in turn.

1. Image

The image of brokers will vary. The Share Centre, for example, has an engaging website (www.share.com) which puts the emphasis on simplicity and domesticity. The home page has a lifelike picture of a cup of steaming coffee and digestive biscuits. The message that dealing is easy is reinforced by a photo of a can of ASDA baked beans. Customers are shown a picture of paint tins and a brush and are told they can give their old PEP a fresh look.

I confess that after perusing this website, I am left with a warm comfortable feeling, much like after strolling down a supermarket aisle with its enticingly arranged display against soft piped music, and the aroma of oven-hot bread.

Oldham says: 'We are at the populist end of the market. The brand is very important and we try to create investor awareness. We don't say we are the cheapest for day traders because our service puts the priority on building relationships, but we are in that ballpark.'

2. Range of services

The online stockbrokers will trade shares. The smaller firms may not deal in stocks on the Alternative Investment Market (see Day 11), and may limit foreign stock trading.

Beyond shares, the range of products on offer varies. The larger firms offer a select range of investment funds, an ISA service, pensions, will-writing and more. Some firms trade bonds, typically by telephone, and perhaps derivatives and foreign exchange.

From around 2005, active traders started migrating to spread betting and contracts for difference (covered on Day 16 and 17), and retail brokers have started to cater for this demand. City Index is the main player in such derivatives trading, and it makes its services available through many brokers.

Some stockbrokers do not welcome the increasing interest in derivatives. The Share Centre is in this category. The only derivatives it offers are covered warrants.

Oldham says: 'Online stockbrokers take on traders in CFDs and spread betting and feel they have gained a client. But CFDs move investors away from cash markets and it is not in the interest of quoted companies. The brokers are selling their birthright for a mess of potage.'

The range of available products has created cross-selling opportunities for the broker, turning them into something of a one-stop financial shopping source for investors. In a typical case, the broker may sell an Individual Savings Account (ISA) to somebody owning shares.

When online brokers act as principal by launching share issues and inviting regular clients to subscribe, there is a potential conflict of interests. Most do not get involved.

3. Dealing costs

Online share dealing services tend to offer cheap dealing. Many still offer commission-free dealing for a limited initial period to attract new customers. The larger brokers often aim to attract frequent and large trades. They may reduce commissions for frequent traders. For example, Barclays Stockbrokers has a set commission of £12 per trade but, when you trade at least 10 times a quarter, it is reduced to £7.50. Some brokers have minimum charges which are cost-effective for larger deals but discourage the smaller ones. This leaves a niche for brokers who want to attract the smaller traders, and who construct their charges accordingly. Halifax Share Dealing offers a facility to buy shares for just £1.50 in commission, where it combines the orders to make a bulk purchase on a set day, four times a month. The Share Centre has a similar batch-dealing scheme, although, according to Oldham, most of its clients choose instead to deal in real time.

Brokers may charge for non-trading services, including portfolio administration, money transfers, having an account and processing share certificates, PEPs and ISAs. 'This type of activity is the highest-value service that brokers have. They should not be giving it away free,' says Oldham.

Experience of US brokers in 2002–3 shows that those that have created such a diversified income stream are more likely to survive a market downturn than those that rely just on trading commissions, he notes.

4. Price of trade

The price at which you buy or sell shares may vary according to the broker's buying power. When, as a buyer or seller, you ask your online broker for a share price, it will relay the request electronically to the retail service provider (RSP), which is the interface between retail brokers and equity markets.

the**share**centre:

when you've turned the last page, turn to us.

Like what you've read? Then let us take you further. We're out to help you confidently turn knowledge into action. In the 'learn' section of our website, www.share.com, you'll find helpful tips about investing, calculators to help you plan your financial goals, a bookshop with the latest titles at discounted prices, and a jargon buster to help explain, for example, that a 'dead cat bounce' is not a veterinary mishap. Then in our 'research' section there are free investment tools including our unique 'SharePicker' and 'FundPicker; and we've even free expert advice at the end of the phone if you want it. So, remembering that the value of investments can go down as well as up and you may not get back what you originally invested, visit share.com or call us. It could be the start of a great new chapter.

- **www.share.com**
- **0870 400 0203**

The RSP will send back the best price it will have determined, with reference to the SETS (Stock Exchange Electronic Trading Service) or SETSmm or to the market makers, mainly through the SEAQ (Stock Exchange Automated Quotation) system. On Day 4, we will look at how these systems work.

The RSP is itself a market maker in some stocks up to a size limit, beyond which it will refer the trade to its own market makers, which provide a service in both quote-driven and order-book securities. Brokers choose how many RSPs they poll; it could be three or it could be a dozen.

The broker may contact several RSPs simultaneously for quotes, and relay only the most competitive one to the client. But some brokers rotate RSPs in turn on the basis of one per deal, which may not achieve so competitive a result. Some brokers may obtain a quote in a deal size other than that requested by the customer. The point to grasp here is that brokers may use different ways to obtain prices from RSPs and the prices may be different. The results may not be equally to your advantage as a trader.

Direct market access

Regular traders of large stocks have good reason to prefer DMA (direct market access) to the RSP route. This way, like the brokers themselves, they make an entry directly onto the LSE order book. It is the only way to place a limit order – specifying the maximum price at which you will deal – that is visible in the market.

If you are to take the DMA route, you must be classified as an *intermediate* customer (from November 2007, professional), which means you will forego some of the regulatory protection given to *private* customers (from November 2007, retail) and you will have to demonstrate that you are a sufficiently sophisticated investor for this.

DMA cuts out the use of a market maker or RSP. You need not worry about the market maker's size limitation. You can put in an order to buy at bid price or below, for as many shares as you want. You will be trading like a market maker yourself. The LSE takes the view that the price improvement obtained offsets by a significant margin the extra cost involved, but some day traders are not convinced.

At the time of writing, iDealing (www.idealing.com) prominently offers DMA, but the vast majority of stockbrokers do not (except through CFDs). 'So far, traders do not know much about DMA but they will be interested once they realize it helps you get a better price,' says Dickinson at Barclays Stockbrokers.

In the long term, Rawlings at Hargreaves Lansdown foresees a shift from the RSP to the DMA model. In the short term, he believes that many brokers will soon start offering DMA but it will appeal only to the higher end of the active trader market. 'Whether most are interested in DMA on equities now is questionable because they trade CFDs or spread bets,' he says. Oldham at the Share Centre calls DMA stillborn. 'DMA has a zonking great charge, which will not be borne by the broker, and the investor would end up paying several pounds a trade, which is as much as the commission.'

DSA (direct strategic access), where the RSP passes unfulfilled limit orders to the LSE order book, has greater growth potential, according to Oldham.

5. Research and news

Research and news coverage are available on the internet for free but if you have all you need on your broker's site, it saves you having to switch between sites.

Brokers typically offer both research and do-it-yourself selection tools with access to raw data. There is demand for either approach, according to Rawlings. Brokers agree that investors are becoming more self-reliant and that research plays a large part in it.

The quality of brokers' research facilities has improved over the years and access is often free of charge. Some brokers offer the basic research free but charge for a premium service. Investor interest in charting facilities is growing.

Level I and II data

Level I data on screen provides basic price data, including the best bid and offer price. Level II data provides individual market maker prices as well as details of pending buy side orders. It enables traders to check on the depth of liquidity in the market and gives them a better feel for how the stock is doing. Access is available from financial websites or brokers.

Brokers are agreed that Level II data is a growth area. At present there are inconsistencies in quality as well as in the monthly charge. I know of one low-priced Level II provider that uses one licence for a number of subscribers, which means that in busy periods some must queue for access.

6. Smooth running and security

The basic online broking service is usually competent these days, but nothing is infallible and you should make what checks you can. If a trade is held up because of system failure or site upgrades, it is *your* money at stake.

Make sure that there is telephone backup, and make a note of the broker's telephone number. Open a backup account with another broker, which will be useful for buying. For selling, it will be more efficient when you have paper certificates. If, as is more usual, you hold shares electronically, and you try to sell them through a broker through which you did not buy, your nominee holdings must be transferred, which creates an administrative hurdle.

Security issues are thankfully no longer the problem they were in the distant past. At the end of 1999, an online broker had a security failure, and clients could gain access to each other's accounts. To avoid this risk, brokers use encryption, which ensures that the information passed between you and the broker online is scrambled. You can only make sense of the information by using the right encryption software and an individual key code. If, as is usual, your broker uses 128-bit encryption, which is the strongest kind, this aspect of security should not worry you.

Make sure that your broker has insurance in place to protect client accounts in case the firm should run into financial problems.

Your broker will have issued you with a password of your choice. Make it a nonsense word, using letters as well as numbers, and keep it secret. While you are in the secure part of your broker's website, do not let anybody watch over your shoulder. Once you have completed a transaction, log out correctly.

7. Limit orders and stop losses

Use a broker that accepts limit orders and stop losses. Limit orders are when you ask your broker to *buy* shares at, or at less than, a specified price, or to *sell* at, or above, a specified price. If your order proves impossible, your broker will cancel the order. Some brokers accept limit orders that they keep open for the day. Others accept them on a fill-or-kill basis, which means they either execute the order immediately, at the price specified, or cancel it.

On Day 14, I will tell you why, if you aspire to a professional level of trading, you should use limit orders. You may apply them to CFDs, spread betting and forex, as well as to shares, and the strategy frees you from the need to watch the market incessantly.

A stop loss is where your stock is sold automatically at a set price level or after a given percentage drop. See Day 14 for more details.

8. Trading hours

All brokers deal during London market trading hours (8.00 am to 4.30 pm, Monday–Friday). You may be able to deal outside market hours. In this case your broker will process your order first thing the following morning, which is when prices of FTSE-100 stocks can fluctuate wildly. Avoid trading out of hours unless you use a limit order.

9. Fantasy trading

Some brokers offer facilities for fantasy or paper trading, which is to go through the motions without committing real money. Your *mock* portfolio may include securities and funds in any combination offered by your broker. You may record the time and date of every mock transaction and whether it was a buy or sell.

The exercise enables you to see your trading history as well as current trades and to learn from your mistakes. But its value has limitations. No mock trade is the same as playing hardball with real money.

A good demo takes you through how to place an order. Many brokers offer this.

10. New equity issues

Your online broker may give you access to new equity issues. Before you take up any offer, read Day 13.

Loyalty is yesterday's game

The services that brokers offer are constantly developing. You should make regular comparisons and be ready to jump ship.

Some large brokers have clients who are loyal because they are longstanding customers of the group's other services. But there is so much competition today that loyalty does not pay, or at least not enough to make it worthwhile.

'The more active the traders, the less loyal they will be to individual brokers and they more they will look for a value-for-money package,' Dickinson at Barclays says.

Broker comparisons

Broker comparisons on the basis of facilities and charges are available from various sources on the web. In updating this book, I found a useful table of different broker charges on the website of AWD Moneyextra (www.moneyextra. com), which is part of the Chase de Vere group. The Motley Fool (www.fool. co.uk) does a comparison table across a span of brokers. As at mid-2006, you could find some interesting personal reviews of stockbrokers at www.chiao. co.uk. Some of the material is out of date, but the leopard does not necessarily change its spots.

Once you have the overview of brokers, there is no substitute for visiting the websites and checking what you get for your money. Do not be afraid to ring up *Customer services* or the equivalent, and ask questions.

The way forward

As an online stock market investor, you are in control. Choose your broker carefully and, if the service is not up to scratch, do not hesitate to move. Investing in shares is about making money and not about keeping everybody happy.

Dynamic rules

■ The larger brokers can often provide better terms, facilities and backup.

■ Direct market access cuts out the use of a market maker or retail service provider and is the only way to place a limit order that is visible in the market. It is not yet popular.

■ Level II data provides individual market maker prices and details of pending buy and sell orders.

■ Open an account with another broker as a backup.

■ Make sure that your broker uses 128-bit encryption software and has insurance in place to protect client accounts.

■ Make the password that you use with your broker a nonsense word and keep it secret to protect client accounts.

■ Place limit orders, particularly if you deal out of hours, and stop losses.

■ Loyalty to an individual broker does not usually pay.

Get a great deal online

You don't have to be an ardent 'ebay-er', 'silver surfer' or budding Bill Gates to know just what an impact the internet has had on our everyday lives. And that's just as true when it comes to investing. Nowadays, the private investor has access to information, news and views like never before – it's all down to the internet.

Access to reliable information and market knowledge, coupled with a good sense of timing, makes for better investment decisions. Whether that's historical information gleaned from studying a company's track record, up-to-the minute knowledge about trading patterns that come from looking at 'live' prices and trading information, or getting your timing right from being able to deal 'there and then', it's all part of the online mix.

But don't imagine online trading is a new fad - brokers report that over half of all 'execution-only' trades are completed online. Nor it is a case of 'take it or leave it' – most brokers combine the many advantages of online trading with more traditional telephone, post or even face-to-face facilities.

Useful places to get details about broker's services include the industry's trade body, APCIM's website (www.apcims.co.uk) and the LSE's own website, (www.londonstockexchange.com). Take a look at some of the comparison and directory sites, like www.find.co.uk or www.moneysupermarket.com too.

What most online brokers will also have in common is the need for you to hold your shares in nominee name. This simply means that instead of your name appearing on the share register, your holdings are registered in the broker's nominee name. But don't worry – you remain the beneficial owner, and your shares are 'ring-fenced' from the broker's own assets, so they are safe and secure. Some offer personal membership of CREST, the market settlement system, so you can still have your name on the register; typically this will incur an extra fee. Either way, it's still a good idea to take a look behind the website – how long have they been around; what's their track record; are they properly authorised and regulated, and members of the appropriate market organisations.

As with many things, the nominee system has pros and cons. It means your chosen broker can carry out your trading for you when you want, with little, if any, paperwork. Typically, they'll look after corporate actions, like takeovers and mergers, and collect your dividends. And they'll send you regular reports detailing your activity, the value of your investments, etc. On the other hand, if you like working your way through a company's Annual Report, voting on shareholder resolutions or attending the AGM then do make sure you choose a broker who will arrange all this for you – because your name isn't on the register you won't receive information direct from the Company. Watch out for shareholder 'perks' too – a few companies won't let brokers pass these on to their investors, and some brokers won't pass them on even if they did.

When it comes to choosing your online broker there are a few other things to consider too. Start with what you want from them. If it's simply an execution service then make sure the site is easy to use, that there's telephone back-up if you can't use it for any reason, and that there is the right level of information and research tools to support your likely trading needs.

If you're likely to want some advice, investment tips or someone to talk over your ideas with, you'll want to be happy its readily available, that they cover the types of investments you'll want advice about and, most importantly, that they 'talk your language'. In effect, that you feel 'at home' with them.

Then there's the question of costs. Online competition has driven down the cost of dealing commission and there's a variety of different charging methods to be found. Comparison sites like Money Supermarket let you input your typical trade and show you how prices compare. Once again, do make sure you've got the complete picture. Are account fees payable and, if so, how much and what do they cover? Can you change your trading tariff if your dealing pattern changes? Are there 'safe custody' fees if you don't trade for a while? What are the costs if, at a later date, you want to transfer your account elsewhere? And, most importantly, are all their charges clearly visible?

Some broker's sites enable you to open an account online, others will require some paperwork, but don't jump at the first site you come to, have a look at what's on offer, call them for a chat, then decide. After all, your online broker's not just for your next trade but will be an important part of your investment life!

The mechanics of dealing online

Overview

In this module we shall look at the process of opening your online account, and the steps you need to take to place your first order. We will focus on the London Stock Exchange trading systems, including the electronic order book and market makers. We will touch on settlement procedure.

First steps

Get online

If you are not online, you will need an internet service provider (ISP) to enable this. Unlimited broadband is now much cheaper than it was and you should have it for fast, cost-effective access.

Update your computer

If your computer is old, or your web browser is out of date, do the upgrades. You cannot afford inferior technology when buying and selling securities. The speed at which you trade may be crucial.

Open your online account

To open your online account, you will need the relevant form, which you can download from your broker's website. Otherwise, e-mail the firm, asking it to send you the form by e-mail.

Once you have printed off the form, fill it in and sign it by hand, as the firm usually prefers a handwritten signature. Send your completed form to the broker. You should enclose money – typically a minimum of £1,000 – to open your account and provide initial dealing funds. You can transfer further funds to and from your designated bank account only.

The firm will issue you as a new client with a welcome pack and password. It will hold your money in an interest-paying account pending your first trade.

Obtain a dealing price

To obtain a price on a stock, you will have to type in the name of the company or, sometimes, its EPIC code, in the box provided. The EPIC code is an abbreviated three- or four-letter symbol which you can look up quickly on your broker's website. Sometimes when you ask for a price, the broker will quote the spread, but when you go through the process of dealing, only the bid or offer price is quoted.

Get your order right

When you place your order, get the numbers right. If you order 30,000 shares when you had intended 3,000, this may not be fully retrievable. If you make such an error, get in touch with your broker immediately – to save time, by telephone. At worst, the broker will probably do a cancelling trade, and you will have to pay the difference in price movement as well as two sets of commission.

Some brokers offer a facility for retracting your order for a few seconds after you have placed it. This can give you peace of mind, but it is irksome for frequent traders as it slows down order placement. Some brokers run an online facility to ensure that you don't spend more on shares than you can afford, or sell shares that you do not own.

Trading systems

We saw in Day 3 that the retail service provider will determine a best price for you on equities with reference to the electronic order book, SETS or SETSmm, or to the market maker system. Let us look more closely at how these trading systems work. Bear with me on the technical detail for the next few paragraphs because it is really worth getting to grips with this.

The London Stock Exchange controls both the electronic order book and the market maker system provided by SEAQ, which is focused on small stocks. In market making there is a small rival system, established in December 2005 by PLUS Markets Group (see Day 11). Let us look in more detail at the order book and market makers in turn.

Order book

SETS, introduced in 1997, is used for trading UK FTSE Euro top 300 securities, which include all securities in the FTSE-100 index, consisting of the largest UK quoted companies, and the most liquid in the FTSE-250, which includes the next largest. Orders entered on SETS compete directly with each other and the system matches buy and sell orders automatically.

In December 2003, the LSE introduced SETSmm, which provides an order-book trading facility for FTSE-250 stocks not already traded on SETS, some dual-listed Irish securities and now the constituents of two smaller company indices, the FTSE Small Cap and AIM 50. SETSmm combines order-book trading with the liquidity backing of market makers, an approach designed to suit those stocks that could not go onto SETS because they were not always liquid enough to get a good pricing mechanism on a pure order-driven system.

SEATS Plus (Stock Exchange Alternative Trading Service) combines an order book with market-maker competing quotes but, unlike on SETSmm, there is no interaction between the two. The system is used for some stocks on the Alternative Investment Market (AIM) (see Day 11), as well as for those on the official list with only one market maker.

Market makers

Market makers make prices and provide liquidity in those shares in which they choose to make a market. The market maker commits itself to providing a price and to dealing in a minimum size, known as normal market size (NMS), throughout the trading day. The firm makes its money on the spread, which is the difference between the bid and offer price. A bid–offer spread of 8–10 means that you can sell to the market maker at 8p or buy at 10p.

SEAQ is the quote-driven market for small- to mid-cap stocks, including on the AIM. Before SETS existed, all UK stocks used SEAQ. Competing market makers display continuous buying and selling prices on SEAQ terminals globally. They set their own prices based on their anonymous proprietary position and their knowledge of order flow as well as on supply and demand.

On the SEAQ screen, a yellow strip shows the most competitive bid and offer price for a given stock. Above it are details such as the previous day's closing quote and trading volume, and the NMS. On the lower part of the screen, *Level 2* information lists every market maker in the stock, with its buying and selling price, which investors may find useful to compare with the current spread.

If the broker is large or has a strong relationship with the firm, it may be able to negotiate a price better than the spread on SEAQ. But most brokers must accept this spread as given. The broker must reveal to the market maker the whole size of any order for which he or she is seeking to transact only a part.

The trend

The LSE has been moving stocks from the 20-year-old SEAQ market-making system to the two-year-old SETSmm order book, partly to meet demand from hedge funds that do electronic programmed trading to exploit arbitrage opportunities. The spreads on SETSmm are tighter and traders need not accept the prices on offer.

An independent review of SETSmm in practice by the ISMA centre at Reading University, completed in February 2005, found that the *headline* touch, the best bid–offer spread, was sharply reduced from the level under the market-maker system, and that transaction costs were significantly reduced. But order-book trading posed problems for many market participants, it found.

The PLUS Service is a quote-driven trading system that was established in December 2005 and competes directly with the other, longer-established systems. Brokers have an incentive to use PLUS if it can access better prices than the incumbent provider and the dealing costs are lower. 'UK investors will want to ensure their broker is accessing the best option available at the time they give them an instruction,' Nemone Wynn-Evans, director of business development at PLUS Markets Group, says.

PLUS has only a tiny percentage of the overall market for share trading but, in its chosen market segment, which is the FTSE Small Cap and Fledgling indices, it has a 15 per cent market share by number of bargains, according to Wynn-Evans. 'This proportion is rising as new brokers come on board,' she says.

Settlement

Once you have dealt, you will need to settle within a specified period, which in February 2001 was shortened in nominee accounts from five to three days. This is known as T+3 and means that both counterparties to a trade agree to *settle* a trade three business days after the trade date, although market makers, as opposed to the electronic order book, can offer some flexibility. If you have share certificates, which are now used only for a small percentage of UK transactions, the settlement period is 10 days (T+10).

In all cases, settlement is electronic, through the CREST computerized system, which matches trades with payments and informs the underlying company's registrar of changes to the share register.

Once you have dealt, you may print your confirmation note off the screen. Keep this as a hard copy. It contains details of the trade and commission charged, as well as stamp duty (charged at 0.5 per cent of purchase value when you buy UK shares, but inapplicable when you sell them).

For more detail on nominee accounts and share certificates, see Day 5.

The way forward

In this short module, we have looked at the mechanics of using your dealer. In the next module we will examine some of the issues that you face as a shareholder.

Dynamic rules

- Your computer technology should be up to date to enable maximum speed. Use broadband.
- If you get the numbers in your order wrong, contact your broker immediately. At worst, your broker will do a cancelling trade and you will pay any costs.
- SETS provides order book trading in FTSE-100 companies, and the largest companies in the FTSE-250. Orders placed compete, and the system matches buy and sell orders automatically.
- SETSmm provides order book trading in some smaller companies, combining it with a market maker approach.
- A market maker commits itself to providing a price and dealing in the NMS throughout the day. It makes its money on the spread.
- SEAQ is the quote-driven market for small- to medium-cap stocks, for which competing market makers display trading prices.
- Settlement of trading of shares through a nominee account is normally T+3, which means three days after the trade date.

The streetwise online shareholder

Overview

In this module, we will look at some of the tasks and choices facing shareholders. We will look at how nominee accounts work and at some of the alternatives. We will focus on dividend payments, rights issues and takeover activity.

We will look at tax considerations, how to diversify your portfolio, and investment clubs. We will finish the module with details of how to complain about your broker and the industry compensation scheme.

Holding your shares

Once you are a shareholder, it is the broker who holds shares on your behalf. The online broker prefers to hold your shares electronically through a pooled nominee account, and some firms insist on this. It is the most usual route and you will have your shares registered in the name of a nominee company run by your broker. You will retain beneficial ownership of the shares, but the underlying company is not even aware that you hold them.

You will not lose access to shareholder perks and voting rights, but it is the nominee company's task to provide you with the relevant information. The company is not even aware that you hold the shares. You will receive dividends and regular account statements.

As an alternative, you may have a CREST-sponsored member account. This means that you will be electronically registered as a CREST member and will incur an annual charge directly from the London Stock Exchange rather than from your broker. When you trade shares, it will be *your* details that are passed electronically with the transaction, but your broker maintains the account on your behalf.

The third alternative is to hold paper certificates, which a minority of investors still prefers. If you are among them, you will need to find a broker that is happy with dealing on this basis, and ideally does not charge highly for it. On completing a deal, you will have to send the certificates through the post, which brings a slight risk of loss.

For active traders, systems are being created to keep all their electronic records in one place, and there are no plans to include paper certificates.

Dividends

As a shareholder, you can often expect a regular dividend (see Day 5) from your shares. This represents a payout from profits to shareholders. Most large quoted companies pay a dividend and many small ones do not, and there is no obligation. Growth companies may find it more useful to reinvest all their earnings in the business and, if it results in a soaring share price, the capital gain for investors may outweigh the dividend income that might have been.

When a UK company makes a dividend payout, it is twice a year and, in the United States, quarterly. It rises a little as Dividend Day approaches, but falls back after the dividends have been distributed and the shares become ex-dividend.

Institutional investors feel comfortable with a steadily rising dividend and, if the momentum stops, they will query it. If a company goes so far as to cut its dividend, it is taken as a warning sign.

Your online broker should put any dividend payment straight into your account, and you can check online that it has been done. At the end of the financial year, the broker will send you a consolidated dividend tax certificate.

Rights issues

A rights issue takes place when a company wants to raise funds from existing shareholders. Unlike dividends, it is not a regular occurrence, but you should be ready for it if it comes. The rights issue gives you as an existing shareholder the right to buy new shares at slightly less than the current value of your existing shares, and without paying a broker's commission.

In a 1 for 2 rights issue, for example, you have the right to buy one new share for every two that you already hold. Alternatively, you can sell your rights in the market, or let them lapse and later receive a cheque from the company for the cash received. Following completion of the rights issue, the share price will even out at slightly below that of your original shares.

Your online broker will inform you of any rights issue for which you are eligible, and you can register any interest by e-mail. But first find out why the company wants the funding. If it is for unwise expansion or another wrong reason, steer clear. Should directors not take up a rights issue, it is often wise to follow their example.

Scrip issues

Your broker will inform you of any scrip issue – also known as bonus or capitalization issue – affecting your holding. A scrip issue is designed to increase the marketability of a company's shares by reducing the share price without compromising aggregate value. It takes the form of an issue of free shares, and there is an accompanying technical change to the company's balance sheet.

After a scrip issue, liquidity of the shares should improve, and you will have more shares but at a proportionately lower share price. The overall value of your holding – unlike after a rights issue – will be the same. In practice, it may rise a little because there is a psychological value attached to having a larger number of shares for the same money.

Takeovers

Your broker should let you know by e-mail of takeover action affecting a company in which you hold shares. If a takeover is to go ahead, the predator must obtain more than 50 per cent of the target company's voting shares. Once its stake has reached 30 per cent, it must make a formal offer to all shareholders. If some shareholders decline to take up an offer, a buyer can acquire their shares compulsorily if holders of 90 per cent of the voting shares have accepted. The acquirer pays for a target company's shares either with cash, its own shares, or a combination of the two.

It is the run-up to the takeover that is the fun bit, and it can also be very lucrative. Companies that are takeover targets, or rumoured to be, may see their share price soar over a short space of time. You can sometimes make a killing if you buy early, and sell out after the share price has risen nicely but before the speculation has subsided. This is a risky trading practice in which timing is crucial and luck plays a part. Don't get greedy and hang on too long. If a takeover rumour is quashed, the share price can drop like a stone.

Tax considerations

Get streetwise about ISAs

Once you have your portfolio in place, you can put your shares in an Individual Savings Account, known as an ISA. This is a government-backed tax-efficient wrapper for your shares and/or other investments. All ISAs must be held in nominee accounts.

The ISA was introduced on 6 April 1999 to replace the PEP and TESSA, and is guaranteed to run until April 2009. To open an ISA, you need to be 18 or over, and normally resident in the UK for tax purposes.

You do not pay capital gains tax on your ISA, but cannot uses losses to offset against gains elsewhere. You will pay no tax on the interest or dividends of your savings within the ISA, but you will pay charges. If you are a basic rate taxpayer you are unlikely to benefit from a stocks and shares ISA, but you will gain from a cash ISA. No minimum holding period or subscription level applies.

There are two types of ISA: maxi ISAs, which must be managed by the same investment company, and mini ISAs, whose components may be managed by different investment companies. Every new tax year, you can have either one or the other.

In any tax year, you may invest up to £7,000 in total, as well as any capital sum from a matured TESSA into a TOISA. In a maxi ISA, you can invest up to the maximum £7,000 (and use a spouse's £7,000 entitlement). Of this you can put anything up to the full amount in stocks and shares, including collective investment schemes and gilt-edged stocks. You can include up to £3,000 in cash provided that you keep to the overall £7,000 limit. A possible combination would be £4,000 in stocks and shares and £3,000 in cash. In practice, most investors in a maxi ISA prefer to invest entirely in the stocks and shares element.

You can invest up to £4,000 in stocks and shares in a mini ISA, again including collective investment schemes and gilts, and up to £3,000 in cash. In both types of ISA, it had been possible to invest £1,000 in insurance, but this was scrapped in April 2005, and the extra £1,000 has been added to the amount that may be invested in the stocks and shares element, as given in the figures above.

The ISA provider cannot reclaim the one-ninth tax credit available on dividend income to prevent double taxation, and so this is effectively wasted. But interest on the funds of corporate bonds is received gross, which is an argument in favour of having this type of bond in your stocks and shares ISA. You will pay no capital gains tax on investments sold from within an ISA, but cannot use losses to offset gains elsewhere.

You can use an ISA to assist in the repayment of a mortgage. You can transfer your ISA directly between two managers, although you may be charged by the new manager.

Capital gains tax

Your capital gains tax allowance for 2006/2007 is £8,500. Only the gains over this level are subject to your marginal rate of tax. Your gain for these purposes is pure profit, which means you may deduct broker costs and the 0.5 per cent stamp duty on share purchases. There is indexation relief on shares held long enough.

If you are married, your spouse will also have capital gains tax relief of £8,500, and you can transfer to your spouse the shares that you wish to sell, making use of annual allowances, and your spouse's tax rate if this is lower than yours. Or you can sell your shares in a year when you pay a low tax rate.

HM Revenue & Customs has abolished the bed-and-breakfast tax loophole where a person could sell shares and buy them back the following day to crystallize gains to offset losses. You can now do a bed-and-ISA, crystallizing a gain, and buying it back in an ISA, subject to its £7,000 tax free limit. You can also do a bed-and-spouse, which is when you sell shares to crystallize a gain and your spouse buys them back.

Inheritance tax

Inheritance tax is payable on your worldly goods after you have died, or after your assets have been transferred by way of gift to a discretionary trust. The rate is 40 per cent on the net value of an estate or gift, after a threshold of £285,000 (2006/2007) up to which you will pay a nil rate. It affects you only if your estate, including the value of your home, is worth more than the exemption.

Diversification

Optimum size

If you buy a poor performing stock, you can offset the damage by having better performers in other sectors. Diversification is about reducing investment risk by not putting all your eggs in one basket. The size of companies in the FTSE-100 index, when measured by market capitalization (share price × number of shares in issue), makes them less risky than most. Be warned, however, that the safety net of size is no longer as strong as it was.

The City accepts that about 14 stocks will give you the maximum benefit from diversification and anything more may reduce effectiveness. Once you have become an old hand at value investing, you will see that it is better to pick five good stocks and put all your money into these, than to go for 10 stocks, of which some are mediocre, and maybe one or two bad.

Asset allocation

Diversification is more effective when it is across asset classes such as bonds, cash, property and commodities, and not just across equities. The idea is to have low correlation between asset classes, so if equities do badly, commodities may do well. The most groundbreaking theory of asset allocation is known as Modern Portfolio Theory, which was published in 1952 in the *Journal of Finance*. Harry Markowitz, the author of the theory, developed the concept of the Efficient Frontier, which is the set of asset distributions that gives the highest returns for any given risk.

If you have the appetite to find out more, visit the online investment library of Seven Investment Management at www.7im.co.uk, where you will find free access to informative and easy-to-read articles about the importance of asset allocation in portfolio construction.

The Weinberg way

Sir Mark Weinberg, chairman at St James's Place, is one of the grand old veterans of the life assurance industry. He founded Abbey Life and, later, Allied Dunbar, both of which became household names. At a conference in May 2006, he said: 'I've been in the investment business 40 years. People collar me at dinner parties and ask what will happen to their Tesco shares or the price of oil. I reply "I haven't the foggiest idea." I don't believe anybody knows because the economy and the world are so full of unknowables.'

In Weinberg's view, investors should follow only the following four rules:

1. Before you invest, have enough liquidity to sleep at nights, and more.
2. Spread and diversify risk, which brings security.
3. Invest for the long term. That way you won't have to worry about what happened in the last 24 hours.
4. If you use money managers, select the best. There are plenty of bad ones.

Bonds

Bonds are loan certificates issued by a government or company to raise cash, and the issuer pays interest at a fixed rate. They are the obvious way to diversify from equities because they are much less risky, and have had long spells of moving in the opposite direction, although more recently this has not happened. One rule of thumb is to invest your age in bonds as a percentage of your portfolio. If you are aged 30, bonds would be 30 per cent of your portfolio but, if you are aged 50, it would be 50 per cent. You can buy bonds from some online dealers but typically by telephone rather than online.

The safest kind of UK bond is issued by the government, and is known as a gilt-edged stock or gilt. Gilt prices tend to go down when interest rates go up because investors in gilts can get better returns elsewhere. Gilts are repaid at their nominal value, and the price moves towards this level as the redemption date approaches.

Gilts are categorized under *Shorts* (under 5 years until maturity), *Mediums* (5–15 years) and *Longs* (over 15 years), as well as *Undated* (no fixed redemption date) and *Index-linked*, which pay a coupon and capital redemption adjusted for inflation according to the Retail Prices Index, and are for risk-averse investors. The longer dated the gilt is, the more its price will tend to fluctuate in line with interest rate changes.

The current yield is the annual interest of the bond, divided by the current price. The lower it is, the higher the gilt price will be, and vice versa. The gross redemption yield is widely used to compare returns on bonds. It is the current yield plus any notional capital gain or loss from the current date to final exemption. If you buy a gilt cum dividend, you will receive the interest payment for the period, and so must compensate the seller. But if you buy ex-dividend, you will not receive the dividend.

Corporate bonds work in a similar way to gilts, but they have a risk of default and so pay slightly higher interest. Investors in corporate bonds face price risk, linked to interest rates, as applies to government bonds, and credit risk, which is the likelihood that the company issuing the bond will fail to pay interest or repay the principal.

Commodities

Commodities have a historical low to negative correlation with equities, which means that they tend to move in the opposite direction, balancing out the portfolio and providing diversification.

You can gain access to commodities through stock market investing. But if you invest in a resource company, for instance, you will be exposed to fluctuation not just in the price of oil but also in the company's own life and in the broad stock market. For diversifying your portfolio, it can be better to gain exposure to pure commodities.

A simple way to do this is through exchange-traded commodities (ECTs), which are listed single securities representing an investment in, or a future on, a commodity. These products track the underlying commodity price, enabling you to take a long or short position as an investor. Another way is through Options (see Day 15).

Investment clubs

In your early days as an investor, two heads can be better than one for avoiding the classic mistakes. It can pay to join an investment club. At the very least, such clubs encourage investors to invest, and take loneliness out of the process.

Members can usefully pool different levels of know-how and life experience, but *only* if they share the same broad view on how to invest. It does not always happen and the club can fail. For instance, technical analysts (Days 8, 9 and 10) have a very different strategy from value investors. The two approaches can be combined but it does not always, or easily, happen.

If you want to be part of an investment club but cannot find a suitable one, consider setting up your own. In the UK, this is easier than you might think. Visit the website of Proshare Investment Clubs at www.proshareclubs.co.uk for help.

You will run your club most easily as a partnership with a legal maximum of 20 members. You will need a treasurer, who issues monthly financial statements, as well as a chairman and secretary. Members will contribute a regular subscription – perhaps £30 a month – to the club's investment fund, and will be entitled to give notice and sell out, removing their stake at its current value. You could hold meetings monthly, ideally in a neutral location such as a pub.

Regulation and complaints

Grounds for complaint

These days, UK-based stockbrokers are authorized and regulated by the Financial Services Authority (FSA). There is substantial emphasis on consumer protection.

One of the key requirements of stockbrokers and other financial services firms is to treat customers fairly – and to show the regulator they are doing it. In general, remuneration should be linked not entirely to volume of trading but also to quality. Products may be expensive but the pricing should be fully transparent. Exclusions in the contract should be mentioned and not just buried in the small print.

Under the UK principles-based regulatory regime, firms must often make key decisions but the FSA holds senior management ultimately responsible for any wrongdoing. It may take enforcement action against all individuals it considers responsible as well as the firm. The industry is very jumpy about this and is likely to address complaints properly. Every stockbroker is required to have a written complaints procedure in place, and you have grounds for complaint if the firm has failed to deal with a complaint competently or honestly.

Financial Ombudsman

If, as a private investor, you should make a complaint and it fails to achieve a satisfactory result within eight weeks, you have access to the Financial Ombudsman Service (FOS), an independent organization with statutory powers to address and settle individual disputes between consumers and financial services companies. The service is financed by a levy on financial institutions.

The FOS is effectively an alternative to the court system. It may use mediation or adjudication to resolve an issue. In the year to 31 March 2005, the FOS investigated 110,963 cases, of which two-thirds were on mortgage endowments, and it gave 55 per cent of them to guided mediation, 39 per cent to formal adjudication and 7 per cent to a final decision by the Ombudsman. The length of time a case takes to resolve depends on its complexity, but six months is usually long enough, according to an FOS spokesperson.

In early 2005, the FOS and the FSA issued a joint consultation. They agreed to make existing complaints procedures transparent and to make access to experts more formally available.

Complain to the press

An unofficial complaint option is to take the matter to the press or TV. Even a threat of this can bring a swift result. If you proceed, I advise you to go to national newspapers or TV, where exposure will hit the firm hardest. You would do well to choose Sunday papers where the journalists have extra time to research their stories. Avoid the populist tabloids. I know people who have talked to them and have, without exception, regarded it as one of the biggest mistakes of their lives.

Whichever complaint route you take, you will be more effective if you have a record of deals and conversations with your broker. Keep notes, and marshal your facts so that you can present them coherently.

Industry compensation scheme

If your FSA-registered stockbroker defaults, you will have access to the Financial Services Compensation Scheme (www.fscs.org.uk), which is funded by the industry. The first £30,000 of any proven claim will be met in full, and 90 per cent of the next £20,000 will be met – with £48,000 being the maximum compensation paid to any single claimant. Overall, the fund will not pay out more than £100 million in any single year.

The way forward

In this chapter we have looked at how to handle your share portfolio, including the various corporate actions. This marks the end of Part 1 of this book.

In Part 2, we will be focusing on ratio analysis and stock selection, using fundamental and technical analysis.

Dynamic rules

- ■ It is most usual to hold your shares electronically through a pooled nominee account. You will retain beneficial ownership of the shares.
- ■ Many UK companies pay dividends. Your online broker will put the twice-yearly payout straight into your account.
- ■ A rights issue gives existing shareholders the right to buy new shares. You should participate only if you feel the company is commercially justified in it.
- ■ A scrip issue is when you are given free shares but the overall value of your holding remains the same. It can give a psychological boost to the share price.
- ■ You can make money trading on takeover speculation. But you need to buy early and to sell out before the speculation subsides.
- ■ An ISA is a government-backed, tax-efficient wrapper for your shares and/or other investments.

- Diversification is about reducing investment risk by not putting all your eggs in one basket. About 14 stocks will give you the maximum benefit across equities.
- Bonds are much less risky than equities but, over the long term, the returns are much lower.
- Commodities move in the opposite direction to equities and bonds, which makes them useful for diversification.
- Should you complain to your stockbroker and fail to get a satisfactory result, you have access to the Financial Ombudsman Service.
- If an FSA-registered stockbroker defaults, you have access to the Financial Services Compensation Scheme.

Part 2

Ratio Analysis and Stock Selection

Fundamentally speaking

For most investors, at one time or another they're going to be looking into the 'numbers' surrounding shares on their 'buy' list. Unlike their earlier counterparts, who'd spend hours pouring over the figures in the Annual Report & Accounts, for online investors crunching the numbers has never been easier.

Many websites exist to provide you with the 'fundamentals' analysis – that group of ratios and performance indicators that are indicative of a share's past, and in some cases, future performance. So now that's its easy to get hold of them, what do you do with them?

The first thing to remember is that a share's performance is relative – it doesn't operate in isolation to what's happening in the global economy as a whole, in the 'local' market in which it is listed or even in isolation to the sector in which the company is engaged.

Some brokers provide ways for you to compare one share's 'fundamentals' with its sector or even with the market as a whole: for instance, The Share Centre's performance Barometers provide an at-a-glance view across 6 parameters.

But fundamentals, despite their name, aren't everything: some shares will go up – or down – when the rest of the market is moving the other way. The 'trick' is to work out why.

Keep in mind that the market is forward-looking – it's not so much interested in what has already happened, but what it thinks will happen in the future. And to complicate things a little further, the share price of any one company will have factored into it a large amount of those expectations. That why, for instance, that a share price can fall on the announcement of what looks like to be good news – record profits, winning a big new contract… It's simply that the expectation was for even better news, so the share price go down. Sometimes this is a 'knee-jerk' over-reaction and it soon comes back, sometimes it isn't.

'Technical analysis' or Chartism is a system many investors subscribe to – the theory goes that by analysing the way in which a share price ahs behaved in the past, you can work out if it's a good or bad time to buy or sell. Fortunately charts are easy to come by – most brokers will provide ready access to them via your online account and many sites make a range of charts available for free. Suffice it to say there are believers and unbelievers – it's worth investing a little time to learn more about the approach before you decide whether or not it's right for you. If nothing else you might find it to be a useful crosscheck of the conclusion you've reached about a share.

But as we've already seen, the numbers aren't everything. In choosing to buy a share always remember that, effectively, you are choosing to buy the business. So as well as looking over the books, look over other aspects of the business too. Is it operating in a sector that's likely to grow? How do its products and service compare with its competitors? Is it an industry where new competition can enter quickly, perhaps with more modern technology or new delivery channels – consider the effect on book and music retailers with the advent of the likes of Amazon and iPods. And what about the management – do they have the experience, expertise and business acumen needed to take the business forward?

All of this may sound daunting, but online investors have access to a multitude of information sources, all aimed at putting information at your fingertips – some for free, others not. Take a look at various websites and services, sign-up for free newsletters, join a few forums and see how you get on. Be selective – you won't want to be overloaded with information. And make sure your chosen sources are reliable…look at their track record too.

All too often investors stick to the financial pages, but keep an eye on the business news too – its covers the broader landscape in which the companies you have invested in have to operate. And you can pick up on trends and changes before they hit the financial pages, giving you a useful head start.

Finally, there's an old adage that 'it takes two to make a market', and indeed it does. The stock market is made up of buyers – those who think the share will go up and give them a good profit – and sellers, for whom the time has come to (hopefully) take their profit and move on. At the end of the day, it's fundamentally a matter of personal judgement and objectives, whatever the numbers say.

How the financial statements work

Overview

As a medium- to long-term investor in a company, you should have some understanding of its financial state, and this is covered by accounting. In this module, we will cover the basics.

Today's accounting environment

The routine

A UK-quoted company issues accounts twice a year. After the first six months of the financial year, whose dates can vary, the company will publish an interim statement. Soon after the full year, it publishes full year figures, known as preliminaries, and, shortly afterwards, the audited report and accounts.

Annual report and accounts

Let us now look at how the annual report and accounts is structured. The first major item is the chairman's statement. It shows the company in the best light, so read between the lines.

At the end of the annual report is the auditor's report. It normally tells you that the accounts are a true and fair representation of the company's financial state. If the auditor qualifies the accounts, it is a warning sign, and you should probably not invest in, or stay invested in, the company.

Sandwiched between the chairman's statement and the auditor's report are, among other things, the three main financial statements: the income statement (also known as profit & loss account), the balance sheet and the cash flow statement. Each statement shows the latest year's figures alongside the previous year's for comparison.

You should read the three statements in conjunction with the notes to the accounts, which are like the small print in a contract. If you do this, you will get as full a picture as possible. Before we take a more detailed look, note that from 1 January 2005, International Financial Reporting Standards (IFRS) came into force for all listed companies in the European Union and, in the next few years, will be adopted in 90 countries.

At present, unlisted companies are allowed, if they wish, to continue to use UK Generally Accepted Accounting Principles (GAAP), but the trend is in the direction of IFRS.

Under IFRS, company accounts disclose more and tend to be longer. Any material error discovered when converting from UK GAAP to IFRS must now have been corrected. Let us look at each of the main IFRS financial statements in turn.

Income statement

The income statement records the company's profits or losses, and how they were reached. At the top is turnover (or revenue), which is all of the ordinary income received by the company. Cost of sales, including production overheads, depreciation and stock changes, is deducted from turnover to show gross profit and, after some other adjustments, operating profit. There is a tax charge, including corporation tax and deferred taxation, which typically amounts to less than the pre-tax profit multiplied by the tax rate. The statement looks something like this:

Consolidated income statement (IFRS style)	£,000
Turnover	x
Cost of sales	(x)
Gross profit	x
Administration costs	(x)
Distribution costs	(x)
Other operating income	x
Operating profit	x

Finance costs	(x)
Share of (loss)/profit from associate	x
Profit before tax	x
Taxation	x
Profit for the year	x
Attributable to:	
Equity holders of the company	x
Minority interests	x

Balance sheet

The balance sheet is another key financial statement and it is best described as a snapshot of the company's position at a given time.

Anthony Bolton, fund manager at Fidelity Special Situations, says that when he has lost a lot of money on a stock, the underlying company has usually had a weak balance sheet. "I now avoid such stocks or take a smaller stake," he says.

On the top half of the balance sheet are the company's assets, which are those items the company owns. They are offset against the company's liabilities, which are what it owes. Total assets less total liabilities equal the net assets of the company. Current assets less current liabilities make net current assets, which is the amount available to pay bills within the year.

Issued share capital and reserves are the shareholders' funds. These, together with any minority interests, are equal to total capital employed.

The key rule of the balance sheet is that a company's total assets equal its total liabilities plus its shareholders' funds. In this way, the balance sheet balances. It looks like this:

Balance sheet (IFRS style)	£,000
ASSETS	
Non-current assets	
Property, plant and equipment	x
Intangible assets	x
Investments in associates	x
Available for sale financial assets	x

Derivative financial instruments	x
Total non-current assets	x
Current assets	
Inventory	x
Accounts receivable	x
Investments	x
Cash and cash equivalents	x
Total current assets	x
Total assets	x
LIABILITIES	
Non-current liabilities	
Accounts receivable/payable in more than one year	(x)
Provisions	(x)
Current liabilities	
Accounts receivable/payable within one year	(x)
Net current assets	x
Total assets less current liabilities	x
Net assets	x
EQUITY	
Capital and reserves	
Issued share capital	x
Share premium account	x
Revaluation reserve	x
Retained profit	x
Minority interests	x
Total equity	x

Cash flow statement

The cash flow statement shows movements in cash and cash equivalents. It is often the part of the accounts that investors and users find most useful because it is not impacted by subjective judgements or assumptions. All cash flows are split between operating, investing and financing items. Profits, as one punter has put it, are a matter of opinion, but cash flows are unchangeable.

The statement starts with cash flow from operating activities. The net figure will be preferably about the same as, or, better still, higher than, the operating profit on the profit & loss account.

Next come investing cash flows, which include those relating to the purchase or sale of long-term assets, and movements in debt or equity in other companies. Interest payments and receipts as well as dividends appear in this section.

Finally we have the *financing* section, which shows how the company obtains cash to finance its operations and related payments. The cash flow statement looks like this:

Cash flow statement (IFRS style)	£,000
Cash flows from operating activities	
Cash generated from operations	x
Interest paid	x
Income tax paid	x
Net cash generated from operating activities	x
Cash flows from investing activities	
Purchase of property, plant and equipment (PPE)	x
Proceeds of sale of PPE	x
Interest received	x
Dividends received	x
Net cash used in investing activities	x
Cash flows from financing activities	
Proceeds from issue of ordinary shares	(x)
Proceeds from borrowings	(x)
Repayments of borrowings	(x)
Dividends paid to minority interests	(x)
Net cash used in financing activities	(x)
Increase or decrease in cash and bank overdrafts	
Cash and bank overdrafts at beginning of year	x
Exchange gains or losses on cash and bank overdrafts	x
Cash and bank overdrafts at end of the year	x

The way forward

This chapter is a bit of a mouthful for non-accountants, and I have kept it as brief as possible. It will help you in understanding financial ratios, as covered on Day 7.

Dynamic rules

■ Listed EU companies must produce IFRS accounts but unlisted companies may still have UK GAAP.

■ The chairman's statement puffs the company. You must read between the lines.

■ Read the three main financial statements together.

■ In the notes to the accounts, you will find the detail that the company does not always want to put in a more obvious place.

■ The income statement records profits and losses.

■ The balance sheet is a snapshot of the company's position on a given day. Assets must equal liabilities plus shareholders' funds.

■ The cash flow statement shows movement in cash and cash equivalents. Profits are a matter of opinion and cash flows are a matter of fact.

Ratio analysis and macro-economic indicators

Overview

This module covers the key financial ratios and should be read in conjunction with Day 6. These will enable you to assess, among other things, how profitable the company is, how much ready cash it has, and how its managers have performed.

I will explain discounted cash flow analysis, which is how professionals most often prefer to value companies. We will look at qualitative evaluation and the impact of macro-economic events.

Become your own analyst

You cannot rely on the professionals

You should always be careful about relying on the judgement of City and Wall Street professionals. With a few exceptions, they are not very good at stock selection, although it does not always diminish their power to move markets. You may check broker recommendations on individual companies at *Times Online* (www.timesonline.co.uk).

You can obtain summaries of analysts' research reports in the magazine *Investors Chronicle*, although bear in mind they are not new and the institutions will have already acted on them.

thesharecentre:

with our free tools to help you make money, what's stopping you?

Investing in the stock market is often seen to be a good way to make money. And, we're out to make it easy to do, with our unique online toolkit including SharePicker and FundPicker – and a free manual to get you started. First, use our free *guide to investing* to help you decide if the stock market is right for you – remember the value of stock market investments can go down as well as up and you may not recover your original investment. Then, explore our website share.com – it's packed with the tools you need to make investing straightforward, including free expert advice on UK shares if you want it. So click on www.share.com or call us now. Because the sooner you get to work on your money, the sooner it can get to work for you.

● **www.share.com**
● **0870 400 0203**

The Share Centre, P.O. Box 2000, Aylesbury, Bucks HP21 8ZB. The Share Centre is a member of the London Stock Exchange and is authorised and regulated by the Financial Services Authority under reference 146768.

Learn the basics of fundamental analysis yourself, so you can understand the output of analysts, and pick, or help to pick, your own stocks. It is what this module is all about.

An investor must examine his or her investment thesis and should be able to explain it to teenagers, according to Anthony Bolton, fund manager at Fidelity. Much hard work is needed to reach this ideal.

It seems that women are better at it than men. One broker has found that women do about 40 per cent more research than men on every trade, according to a June 2006 white paper on spread betting commissioned by Finspreads and prepared by two academics from Cass Business School.

Ratios

You can pull ratios from figures in the accounts, or you can find them made up for you in any newspaper or on financial websites and software. They enable you to value companies on fundamentals against their own past and their peers. But if the same ratio for two companies was calculated differently, the differences must be reconciled to make a like-for-like comparison.

Let us now look at some key ratios.

Earnings per share

The earnings per share (EPS) is a measure of the company's profitability. It is the profit attributable to the ordinary shareholders (ie profit before ordinary dividends) divided by the number of ordinary shares in issue during the year. The City looks for an EPS that rises steadily, even if slowly, year by year, and rewards companies that can demonstrate it.

Listed companies are required to disclose two measures of EPS, basic and diluted, on the front of the profit & loss account. The diluted EPS figure adjusts the basic EPS figure to show what the result would have been had all potential ordinary shares (such as employee share options and convertible debt) been converted into shares.

Companies can also provide an adjusted EPS figure but in the notes to the accounts and not on the face of the profit & loss account. The adjusted figure may show earnings before items that the directors prefer to exclude.

Price/earnings ratio

The price/earnings ratio is the share price divided by earnings per share. It is how the market rates a stock and shows how many years it will take the company, at the applicable rate of earnings, to earn the equivalent to its market value.

If the company's P/E ratio is low compared with that of its peers, the shares are looking cheap. They could be good value, but are very likely to be depressed for a reason.

If the company's P/E ratio is high compared with that of its peers, the shares are looking expensive, but it could be for a good reason.

The historic P/E is listed in the newspapers and, to find the sector and market averages for comparison purposes, you should look at the FT's Actuaries Share Indices (The UK Series) in Monday's *Financial Times*.

The prospective P/E is more up to date than the historic figure because it is based on the future analysts' earnings forecasts, but is also less reliable because they can be wrong.

The P/E ratio can tell you something about the broader market. In the five years to mid-2006, the P/E ratio steadily fell in Britain but French and German P/E ratios ended up slightly higher, according to analysts. *The Times* said in a leading article on 3 July 2006 that a growing gap between the UK and its European competitors had to raise serious questions about how the market was judging the British economy.

The P/E ratio has limitations. It does not take account of a company's earnings growth, which is important for small companies.

A PEG to hang your valuation on

The price/earnings growth ratio, known as PEG, redresses the balance by combining an assessment of growth with the P/E ratio, and is used to value small growth companies. The ratio is calculated, either on an historical or prospective basis, as the P/E ratio divided by the average growth rate of earnings per share.

Investment guru Jim Slater has advocated a PEG of well under 1 as a criterion for selecting growth. If a company has a prospective P/E ratio of 10 and earnings per share growth of 20 per cent, the PEG ratio is 10 divided by 20, which is 0.5 and, on Slater's criterion, very attractive. A stock with a prospective P/E of 30 and earnings per share growth of 15 is on a PEG of 2, which he finds too high.

Net assets

To value property companies, investment trusts or composite insurers, use the share price/net asset value (NAV) per share. This is the company's total assets less its liabilities, debentures and loan stocks, divided by the number of shares in issue.

If a company is trading on a low share price/NAV, it may be a bargain, or have problems that are not easily resolvable and that make it a poor investment.

Check how the net asset figure is made up. Properties historically valued on the balance sheet may be worth more because of subsequent capital gains. Machinery may be valued too low owing to a conservative depreciation policy (see box below).

Depreciation

Depreciation is the gradual reduction in value of a fixed asset as it is used by the business over its useful life. It is expressed as an annual deduction from the income statement. For intangible assets, amortization is used instead.

Companies have a choice in how they calculate depreciation. The method they choose will have its own impact on reported profits. Companies should use a consistent method unless there is a good economic reason for changing.

In practice, there are two common methods of depreciation for UK companies. The most popular is the *straight line* method, which spreads the cost of the asset equally over its expected economic life. For example, a company may depreciate an asset valued at £10,000 by reducing its value by £1,000 annually over 10 years.

The second most popular way to depreciate assets is the *reducing balance* method. This way the asset's value is reduced annually by a given percentage.

Gross yield

The company's gross yield is the gross annual dividend expressed as a percentage of the share price. It is useful for comparing companies in terms of income.

The more a company's share price falls, in reflection of poor perceived prospects, the higher the gross yield rises. Stocks out of favour may have high yields, and there is a school of contrarian investing that favours buying them.

High yield investing can backfire because too many of the stocks are duds, although, across blue chip companies over the long term, the method has often outperformed the market average.

Dividend cover

Dividend cover is how well earnings cover dividend payments. It is calculated as earnings per share divided by dividend per share. If it is not at least one, the dividend is not covered by the company's earnings and the company may dip into reserves to maintain or increase it, so keeping up appearances. The problem may be temporary, or the slippery slope towards a dividend cut, and city analysts may be relied on to draw attention to it.

Current and quick ratio

Liquidity is how much cash a company can lay its hands on at short notice. The way to check this is the current ratio, which is the company's current assets divided by current liabilities (figures available on the balance sheet). As a rule of thumb, this should be at least two.

The quick ratio, known colloquially as the *acid test*, is a more stringent liquidity test. It is current assets less stock and work-in-progress, divided by current liabilities. It should ideally be over one.

Enterprise value/EBITDA

Quoted companies in the high-tech and telecommunications sectors may have neither yield nor earnings and be paying interest on substantial debt. In their own sectors' terms they may be great companies, or potentially so, but some are not. Analysts prefer to use valuations suitable for such companies, and a favourite is the EV/EBITDA ratio.

The EV is enterprise value, which is market capitalization (share price × number of shares in issue) plus debt less cash. The EBITDA is earnings before interest, tax, depreciation and amortization.

The usefulness of EV/EBITDA is that it ignores the interest payment burden of debt, which is typically heavy in the sectors to which the ratio is applied. The EBITDA concept was used by analysts to value WorldCom, the US telecommunications group where, in June 2002, a US~$11 billion accounting fraud was revealed. A month later, the company made a bankruptcy protection filing. Analysts then stopped using EBITDA as a standalone stock valuation tool. But it is still considered very valuable, and Anthony Bolton says that it is one of the ratios he scans in stock picking for his Fidelity Special Situations Fund.

Return on capital employed

The return on capital employed (ROCE) is a widely used measure of management performance. It may be calculated as profit before interest payable and tax, divided by year-end capital employed, which consists of total assets less total liabilities excluding long-term loans.

The higher a company's ROCE, the better the company is at using the assets at its disposal. Ideally, the ROCE should be rising year-on-year.

Gearing

The gearing ratio expresses the company's level of borrowing. It is the percentage of interest-bearing loans and preference share capital, divided by ordinary shareholders' funds. As a rule of thumb, if gearing is over 50 per cent, it could be cause for concern.

Price/sales ratio

It is pointless trying to apply the P/E ratio to small companies that have not yet shown a profit because the earnings component will be nil. In such cases, the price/sales ratio (PSR) can be an alternative and it is often used for high-tech growth companies.

The PSR is calculated as market capitalization divided by last year's sales. The PSR could be as low as five or six, or as high as 30 or 40 and, if it is low, it could represent value. The only way to assess whether the ratio is too high or low is by comparing it with that of the company's peers.

Discounted cash flow analysis

Discounted cash flow (DCF) analysis is the single most widely relied-on technique of securities analysts for assessing a company's prospects. The process involves looking at likely future cash flows and translating them into present day value. To achieve the appropriate discounting, the analyst must take into account the time value of money.

Let us look at how you discount future cash flows, for which you will need the company's financial statements to hand. You will start with the company's net operating cash flow (NOCF), which you may find as follows.

Take the company's earnings before interest and tax. Deduct corporation tax paid and capital expenditure, and add depreciation and amortization, which do not represent movements in cash. Add or subtract the change in working capital, including movements in stock, in debtors and creditors, and in cash or cash equivalents. This is the year's NOCF. It can be calculated for future years, and reduced in value to present day terms by a discount rate.

For DCF purposes, cash flows are likely to continue beyond the period over which it is possible to assess cash generation accurately. This can be modelled through use of terminal value. Present and future modelled cash flows, together with the terminal value, make up the net present value (NPV) once they have been discounted at an appropriate cost of capital. The number of years over which these cash flows are discounted, and the actual future NOCF forecasts, will influence the NPV. Besides this, the larger the discount rate used, the smaller is the NPV.

Weighted average cost of capital (WACC) is often used as the discount rate. Generally, companies raise their capital through equity or debt. The WACC represents the cost of capital to the company weighted in terms of debt and equity. We can break down the WACC into its two components. First, the cost of debt is the current yield to maturity on the company's bonds. Second, the cost of equity is commonly measured by the Capital Asset Pricing Model (CAPM – pronounced CAPEM).

The CAPM finds the required rate of return on a stock by comparing its performance with the market. It expresses this return as equal to the risk free rate of return plus the product of the equity risk premium and the stock's beta. The formula is as follows:

Cost of equity = risk free state + (equity market risk premium × equity beta)

The CAPM assumes that the market rewards investors for acquiring investments which carry a larger amount of *market* risk, which cannot be diversified away. The higher a share's market risk, the higher is its so-called beta. If a share fluctuates in line with the market, it will have a beta of 1.0. If it has a beta of 2.0 or 0.5, it will fluctuate at twice or half the market level respectively.

Unfortunately, beta is an historical figure and so not always reliable, so a portfolio of high-beta stocks does not always outperform one of low-beta stocks as it should. In practice, beta works better over a period – decades rather than years – or at times of major share price fluctuation such as during a market crash.

According to the CAPM, investors are not rewarded for taking unsystematic (ie company-specific) risk because it can be eliminated through diversification. This is in keeping with Modern Portfolio Theory from which the CAPM originates.

The CAPM is a theoretical model. It assumes no taxes or transaction costs, and that investors see the same investment opportunities and have a shared time horizon and expectation of return. It assumes that investors may borrow and lend at the risk-free rate of return and that investments are properly and instantly priced according to risk levels, and that market information is made available instantly and free of charge to all investors. In the real world, the theory is used extensively, and adjustments can be made where the assumptions fall short of the reality.

Several models

To make forecasting more likely to take into account unforeseen events, analysts may plot DCF models using several discount rates to present alternative valuations. This approach is more useful analysis than attempting a single DCF forecast. It acknowledges that DCF analysis cannot always predict the future, and it reduces the scope for abuse. In the past, analysts have abused the DCF concept to promote favoured companies on the basis of inflated expectations, a practice that recent regulatory trends have made much more difficult.

Qualitative factors

Some value investors focus purely on ratio and DCF analysis, but it makes sense to mix these with qualitative assessment.

Warren Buffett and Anthony Bolton, as value investors, take the view that the franchise is more important than the management. An average manager could run a great franchise and a great manager could not do much with a bad one, according to Bolton.

History shows that management with a strong track record can help steer the company through difficult times. Check the age of key managers. If the chief executive is in his late forties, he or she is young enough to stay with the company for the foreseeable future, but mature enough to have experience and judgement. Much older or much younger could lead to problems, although there are plenty of exceptions.

Steer clear of companies where managers have been linked with failure or fraud. Bolton says: 'I used to think that if the business was good but there's a question mark about the management's integrity, I'll buy. I've changed my mind.'

Macro-economic events

Be alert to macro-economic events that will affect the stock market. The key issue is inflation, which may be broadly defined as the continued rise in price levels that diminishes the value of money.

The Chancellor of the Exchequer, acting for the Treasury, sets the annual target for inflation, currently 2 per cent a year, as measured by the Consumer Price Index. The Bank of England has the task of keeping it to that level and, with this in mind, it has established a Monetary Policy Committee (MPC) to decide whether to change the *repo* rate. This is the short-term rate at which the Bank lends to banks for repurchase agreements. It is for practical purposes synonymous with *base* rate.

If the Bank of England announces that it will be cutting interest rates, this stimulates the stock market as well as the broad economy. It means cheaper borrowings for quoted companies, and many people will buy shares rather than leave their money on deposit for a lower return. If the Bank of England raises interest rates, it is, broadly speaking, to curb inflation and this will adversely affect shares.

If the stock market is surprised by an interest rate move, it will overreact. More often than not, it will have expected the move and will have *discounted* it in advance. In this case, it will react not strongly, if at all. Generally, the Bank of England tries to signal future rate changes. The MPC will have made its decisions using inflationary indicators. Here are some of the key ones:

■ *Consumer Price Index (CPI).* This is the measure used by the UK government since December 2003 to set its annual inflation target.

■ *Gross Domestic Product (GDP).* This measures national income and is revised quarterly. If GDP rises over 3 per cent in each of four quarters in succession, it sends a strong inflationary warning and the Bank of England will probably raise interest rates.

■ *Index of Production.* This monthly time series measures the volume of production in manufacturing, mining and quarrying, and energy supply industries.

■ *Money supply.* Monetarists, unlike Keynsians, believe that the money supply is the key to controlling inflation. Their views are currently out of fashion. UK money supply measures include M0, which represents narrow money – money in circulation plus sight deposits (current accounts with money available on demand), and M2, which is broad money – M0 plus savings deposits and time deposits.

■ *Monthly unemployment count.* If unemployment is falling, it benefits companies that rely on consumer spending. But it may lead to a rise in interest rates to combat rising inflation fears.

■ *Producer prices.* The Producer Price Index (PPI) measures price changes in goods bought and sold by UK manufacturers. It is based on a weighted basket of goods.

■ *Purchasing Managers' Index.* This seasonally adjusted index, known as PMI, provides a view of the manufacturing economy.

■ *Retail Price Index.* The Retail Prices Index measures the price rises in a basket of goods, based on prices collected locally and centrally, with a random sampling of locations. The headline RPI has derivations, one of which is the RPI-X, which is the headline figure excluding mortgage rates. The RPI and its derivations are used for the indexation of pensions, state benefits and index-linked gilts.

■ *The state of sterling.* If sterling is strong, imported commodities, on which the UK relies heavily, are cheaper. This helps to keep inflation down.

Fundamental data resources

You do not need to pay for fundamental data. A lot is available free from your broker and financial websites. But if you are willing to pay a subscription, you can obtain the most valuable information you need in a single integrated source, which can save you time. In mid-2006, the London Stock Exchange (www.londonstockexchange.com) introduced a new service, Company Report, which, for £10, gives you a report providing fundamental data, directors' dealings, broker estimates and similar on a company, giving insight about its past performance and future prospects.

Investment software should give you access to company statistics and prices, including highs and lows, and charts as well as news flow. It should enable you to set stop losses and alert you when these are reached, as well as calculate your tax liability. You should be able to create a number of portfolios simultaneously, and to liaise with other users.

To find the software that is right for you, invite the promoter to send you samples or to provide a live demo. Check views on the online bulletin boards. For investors with limited experience, Sharescope software (www. sharescope.co.uk) is an excellent choice. Real-time prices provision sends up the subscription prices. So do some less widely used features. Try to pay only for what you need.

Imaginative presentation can help you to grasp the meaning of statistics more quickly and clearly. Many investors value the quarterly updated book or CD ROM provided by Company REFS (Really Essential Financial Statistics) (www.company-refs.co.uk). This product conveys the key messages from a wide range of statistics through lunar symbols. The more black there is as a slice of a moon, the better the statistic. A very low P/E ratio is welcome and will attract a moon covered in black, but a very low return on capital will have it covered in white. Jim Slater was a driving force in developing this product.

The way forward

This and Day 6 are the most important modules in this book. Accounting is the language of business and, as an investor, you will be at a huge disadvantage if you do not have some understanding of it.

Dynamic rules

- Keep an eye on analysts' forecasts. Whether right or wrong, they can move markets.
- The City rewards companies that achieve a readily rising earnings per share.
- The P/E ratio is how the market rates a company. It shows how many years it will take the company, at the present rate of earnings, to earn its market value.
- The PEG ratio combines an assessment of earnings growth with the P/E ratio and is used to value small growth companies. The lower it is, the better.
- Use net asset value per share to value property companies, investment trusts or composite insurers.
- Depreciation is the gradual reduction in value of a fixed asset. Companies should use a consistent method.
- Growth companies can often make more money for investors by reinvesting earnings than paying a dividend.
- If a company that regularly pays a dividend cuts it, this is a danger sign.
- A company needs a current ratio (current assets less current liabilities) of at least 2 to demonstrate adequate liquidity.
- EV/EBITDA may be used to value high-tech/telecoms companies with high interest payments.
- Dividend cover is earnings per share divided by dividend per share and it should be at least 1.
- If a company's gearing (borrowing) exceeds 50 per cent, it is time to ask questions.
- If a company has a rising return on capital employed, it is using its assets efficiently.
- The price/sales ratio is commonly used to value technology companies without earnings.
- Analysts favour discounted cash flow analysis to value companies. It is best calculated on several discount rates.
- Invest in market-leading companies with strong, experienced management, and growth potential as well as value.
- A cut in interest rates benefits shares, and a rise has the opposite effect.

- The Consumer Price Index is used by the UK government to set its inflation target.
- Gross Domestic Product measures national income.
- Money supply is believed by monetarists to control inflation.
- Falling unemployment benefits consumer spending but may lead to a rise in interest rates to combat a perceived inflation threat.
- If sterling is strong, imported commodities are cheaper, which helps to keep inflation down.

Charts galore

Overview

In this module, we will consider how technical analysis works, the pros and cons, and the types of chart in use.

The theory of technical analysis

How technical analysis works

By now you may have recognized a theme running through this book, that value investing works well in the medium to long term but not necessarily in the short. In trading and short-term investing, timing is crucial and technical analysis can help with it.

Technical analysis involves the study of past share prices or indices and, for timing purposes, is helpful in showing you when a stock price is out of kilter with the past. There are technical systems for setting stop losses and assisting with money management, which is a crucial part of trading (see Day 14).

The dedicated technician analyses the charts and indicators to forecast future share price and index movements. Some use technical analysis as an alternative to fundamental analysis, and cynics say it is popular because it is easier to understand than company accounts. Nobody could accuse investment software providers of not rising to the challenge.

There are technicians who apply their art in its purest form, and take pride in reaching conclusions based only on share price movements, without knowing the surrounding events or the stock fundamentals. If several patterns and indicators point to the same outcome, it is much stronger than if only one is behind it. Some use technicals to support, but not replace, fundamental analysis. Fidelity fund manager Anthony Bolton is in this camp. Trader Alpesh Patel believes both are valid, and the proportions of use depend on the investor's own comfort zone.

However much it is used, technical analysis remains controversial. Among experts, the critics are more numerous than the supporters. They say that past share price movements do not repeat themselves in the same form, on the same time scale, and that most technicians make little money.

The true technicians dispute it. US share trader Marty Schwartz used fundamental analysis for nine years and it did not work well. He switched to technical analysis and became rich. US fund manager William O'Neil said: 'Just as a doctor would be foolish not to use X-rays and ECGs, investors would be foolish not to use charts.'

What is not in dispute is that it is possible to earn a living writing and lecturing about technical analysis, and making technical forecasts. The more publicity technical analysis receives, the more trading it generates, which helps the cause. Cynics say that technical analysis becomes a self-fulfilling prophecy.

Some of the penny-share promoters relish the fact that technical analysis may be applied to newish companies with no track record as much as to those with better fundamentals. It means more investor interest.

Dow Theory

Dow Theory is behind most of modern trend theory. Financial journalist Charles Dow started developing the Theory in the late 19th century after he noticed that stocks tended to rise or fall together. He introduced, and based Dow Theory around, two stock market indices: the Industrial Average, which consisted of 12 blue chip companies, and the Rail Average, which had 20 railroad companies.

Dow Theory says that the share price reflects *everything* that is known about a stock. There are three trends in the stock market and they may all be operating simultaneously.

The primary trend lasts between one and several years in three phases, and to assess it is the priority for successful speculation, according to Dow Theory. The secondary trend lasts from about three weeks to three months and retraces between one- and two-thirds of the gain or loss on the primary. A tertiary or minor trend lasts for between one day and three weeks and shows daily fluctuation. It is significant only for very short-term traders.

One way in which a trend will end is when the share price fluctuates for two to three weeks within a five per cent range, which creates a line. The longer and narrower the line, the more powerful will be the breakout. To validate Dow

Theory, the line should arise on either or both of the Industrial and the Rail Averages, depending on which version you follow. If it is on both indices, the message is stronger, and which gave the first signal is unimportant.

Trading volume counts but is a secondary consideration, according to Dow Theory. An overbought market has lower volume on rallies and higher volume on declines. An oversold market has the reverse.

Taken over the first half of the 20th century, shares bought on Dow indications beat the market massively, even after trading expenses. But Dow Theory is not infallible, and was never intended to be. Its signals come late, which means that early potential profit is reduced. The Theory attracts the criticism that it is out of date but the loyal say that the Averages have modern equivalents.

Different kinds of chart

Charts come in many shapes and sizes. They can be daily, weekly or monthly. They may be plotted on a semi-logarithmic scale, which shows share price or index movements in percentage terms, putting them in scaled perspective. Alternatively, charts may be plotted on the arithmetic, or linear, scale, which emphasizes absolute share price movements, and so presents a more sensitive picture, which is useful if the price range tends to move only slightly.

You may find volume displayed at the bottom of charts in the form of vertical bars, or in a separate chart. The display is usually on a relative adjusted volume basis, with the bottom of the bars showing the lowest volume traded, rather than none, which makes it easy to detect uncharacteristic trends.

Because charts are widely available in computerized form, you do not need to plot them by hand but some technical analysts prefer this longer route because it keeps them focused on the detail.

The most widely used types of chart are the line chart, the bar chart, Japanese candlesticks, and the point-and-figure chart. Let us look at each.

Line chart

The line chart is useful for charting long-term trends. It has a line that plots price on the Y axis against time on the X axis over a period of your choice, whether five minutes or a week.

The closing mid-price is typically used. It eliminates the *noise* of intra-day share price volatility, which arises in the bar chart. On the line chart, it is easier to spot trend changes.

Bar chart

This gives the technician more detailed information than a line chart. The share price is similarly plotted against time. For each time period, a bar is drawn, the top of which represents the high during the period, and the bottom the low. On the left of the bar, a tick shows the opening price and, on the right, a tick shows the closing price.

The bar chart can appear cluttered, but charting software enables you to zoom in on a part of it. The scale is most often arithmetic.

Candlesticks

The Japanese were using candlesticks, also known as candles, more than 100 years before technical analysis started in the United States. It is only recently that they have become popular in the West. This is largely thanks to candlesticks guru Steven Nison, who has published pioneering books on the subject.

The candlestick, as it appears on the chart, is based round a vertical line that extends from the high to the low of the share price (or of any other instrument used) over the given period, which is usually a day. One horizontal line crosses

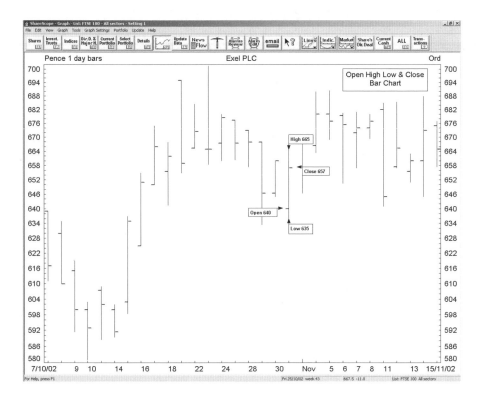

this vertical line at the stock's opening price, and another crosses it at the closing price, making a vertical rectangle which, in candlesticks terminology, is the *real body*.

If the price at close was higher than at opening, the real body is white and, if the price was lower, the real body is black. There may be shadows, which are vertical lines above or below the real body. The straight line above it is the upper shadow and that below it the lower shadow. The shadows represent any price action that extended beyond the opening or closing price.

The contrast of black with white provides visual power, and the patterns often have graphic names, such as Hammer or Morning Star or, in Japanese, Harami, which means pregnant woman (or body within).

Candlesticks, unlike bar charts, are usable only when an opening share price is available because they focus on its relationship with the closing price. They do not indicate the likely extent of a turn and so are not used by technicians to set price targets. Candlesticks give more priority to *reversal* than *continuation* signals, and signal a reversal faster than Western trend analysis or moving averages (see Day 10). They traditionally ignore volume and trend lines, although the software is incorporating these as innovations.

Given the profile, candlesticks are best used for examining share price movements over a short period, which is useful for traders but not so much for medium- to long-term investors.

Not everybody is convinced about candlesticks. Many years ago, when I was a student on courses run by the Society of Technical Analysts, I encountered some high-level feeling against the concept, and I know of one candlesticks instructor who has never used it in his own trading. The flip side is that there are plenty of candlesticks enthusiasts, including Tom Hougaard, chief market strategist at City Index.

To find out more, visit Candlecharts.com, the website of Steve Nison at www.candlecharts.com. It is impossible not to enjoy the website of this maestro. See Day 20 for details of Nison's seminal book. Another useful site is Lit Wick at www.litwick.com, which has a good glossary of bullish and bearish indicators in candlesticks. The sites provide some – hem – illumination.

Point-and-figure chart

The point-and-figure chart, even more than the line chart, cuts out noise extraneous to pure share price movement, and focuses on trends. The Y axis

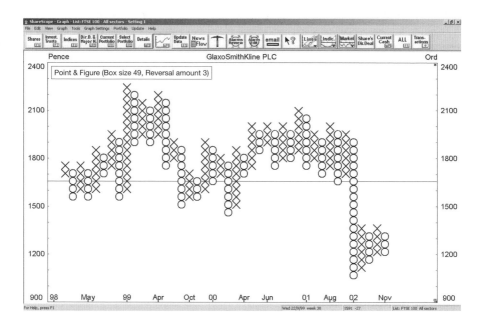

represents price, the X axis measures time, and prices are plotted only when a significant and pre-decided level of change has taken place.

Let us suppose that 10p is the required level of change on a point-and-figure chart representing a stock price. This measure of change is known as the box. In an upward trend, every time that the share price rises by 10p, an X will be marked. In a downward trend, whenever the price falls by 10p, 0 will be marked.

To provide a time scale, the month's first entry on the chart may be recorded as the initial letter of the month, such as 'F' for February. On computer-generated charts, upward-pointing chevrons may be used for price rises, and downward-pointing chevrons for price falls.

Should the share price break the trend and change direction, it will need to register a reversal before the movement is recorded on the chart. The reversal is often larger than the box size. If it is three times as big, it will be known as the 3-box reversal. In an upward reversal, an X will be marked, changing from a 0. In a downward reversal, a 0 will be marked, changing from an X. In either case, a new column will have been opened, which starts one square across.

Some technical analysts use a method known as the Count to forecast share price movements. It requires you to check how many reversals show on the chart. The more there are the bigger the anticipated breakout, according to the theory.

If the box and reversal are small, the number of X and 0 columns tends to be large. Such a chart may cover a day's trading. If the box and reversal are bigger, the columns will be fewer and the chart may cover weeks or even months. To conduct a thorough analysis of a single stock using point-and-figure, it is desirable to have several charts, each with a different fraction of the box size normally applied to the stock. For long-term observation, you could have a 50 per cent box size, and, for the medium term, as little as 25 per cent.

The point-and-figure chart, unlike candlesticks, is not helpful for short-term trading. It is harder to understand than the line or the bar chart, according to trader Harry Schultz. But Jeremy du Plessis, dubbed the UK's most qualified technical analyst, favours the point-and-figure chart because he can become intimately engaged with it. David Fuller, another leading technical analyst, has made point-and-figure his prime area of focus.

To find out more, visit the informative website of Dorsey Wright Associates (www.dorseywright.com), an advisory service that specializes in this type of charting. Register with the site and you can go on a free course at its online Point and Figure University.

The way forward

Technical analysis tends either to grab you or not. For enthusiasts we have the next couple of modules to explore the concept in more detail.

Dynamic rules

- Technical analysis is based on an unproven premise that past movements repeat themselves, but it can become a self-fulfilling prophecy.
- The line chart provides less information than the bar chart, but cuts out *noise* and is useful for charting long-term trends.
- The point-and-figure chart focuses on even more significant share price movement.
- Japanese candlesticks are for short-term traders and are not used for setting price targets.

How technical analysis can make you money

Overview

In this module, we will focus on how technical analysis can make you money. We will look at how you can profit from trend theory, set support and resistance lines, and use trend channels for trading. We will see how continuation and reversal patterns work, the likely extent of a breakout and the trading implications. We will check out Fibonacci numbers and Elliott Wave theory.

How to use the charts

The trend is your friend

Technical analysts dispute many finer points of their craft but are agreed on the premise that the share price moves in trends. The usual advice to investors is to go with the flow. An uptrend in the share price shows that demand is greater than supply, and you should buy the shares for as long as it lasts. Conversely, if the trend is down, you should sell the shares or go short on them, again until the trend reverses.

The longer a trend lasts, the more reliable it is likely to be, technical analysts are agreed. Trends remain in force until they are broken, when a charting software package may be programmed to trigger an alarm.

A trend may be in many time frames simultaneously and the short-term trend is more likely to continue if it is moving in the direction of the longer-term one, technical analysts say.

Victor Niederhoffer, a US trader and author, has challenged whether the trend exists. In so doing, he has attacked the concept of technical analysis at root.

Support and resistance

The *resistance* level is the high point on a chart where the stock price has stopped rising, because investors will not buy further and sellers have emerged. At the other extreme, the *support* level is where investors have stopped selling.

The more a support or resistance line is tested, the more effective it is considered. Support and resistance often arise at round numbers which, in the case of stocks, are often 90p, 100p or 200p.

Trader David Jones explains to packed seminars in London how he uses support and resistance to help time his own trades. 'If a share price rises above the resistance line, you buy, and if it goes below the support line, you sell. This works for any market,' he says.

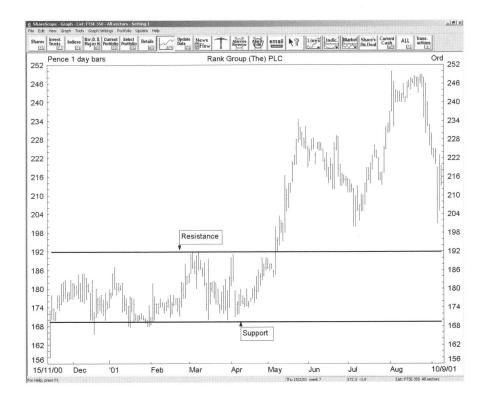

the**share**centre:

the better you're informed
the easier your decision.

Picking shares is more straightforward when you can see both sides of the story. That's why The Share Centre has designed the Performance Barometer. It shows you, at a glance, how a company's shares are performing relative to their sector and the FTSE All-Share – measured against six key investment criteria. So you'll know whether it's worth pursuing further. Our Performance Barometer and other online research tools are all designed to help make choosing shares easier. And every account comes with free expert advice over the phone too. Of course, share prices can go down as well as up, and you may not recover your original investment, but by using our performance barometer you could end up with the pick of the crop, instead of just grasping at straws.

● **www.share.com**
● **0870 400 0203**

The boundaries are self-renewing and, once the share price has fallen below the support level, it becomes the new resistance line. It makes sense because some of the shareholders who failed to sell before the share price fell below the old support line will seize the opportunity if the price should subsequently return there. It works both ways and the resistance level after the share price has risen above it becomes the new support level.

Trend channels

Once a trend has three tops or bottoms in succession, a *trend line* may be drawn against them, and it confirms the trend. A trend channel is the space between a trend line touching the highest points, indicating resistance, and a parallel line touching the lowest points, indicating support.

In the case of a volatile stock, the trend channel will be large enough to trade profitably on price fluctuations *within* it. It brings a whole new meaning to the term *cross-channel shopping*. Some traders divide the trend channel along the middle with a horizontal line and, when the share price is above it, they sell the shares, and when it is below, they buy them.

Chart patterns

Many are sceptical about reading meanings into patterns in the charts. The pattern is the most famous manifestation of technical analysis. It appears on any type of chart but is clearest on the line chart. Any pattern is constructed from the price fluctuation on the chart representing the struggle between buyers and sellers. The pattern repeats itself in different markets and on different stocks.

Every pattern shows how the dynamics of supply and demand play out, and technicians believe that it has some predictability. Some use the patterns to time trades and predict future price movements, and others are cynical, even sometimes from within the ranks of technicians.

When one side gets the upper hand, the line breaks out of the pattern. On an upside movement, trading volume tends to rise. As a rule of thumb, the move is confirmed only when it has exceeded 3 per cent of the share price, and there are many false breakouts.

If a breakout happens, there is a neat, if not wholly reliable, rule on how long it should last. Measure the full depth of the preceding pattern and project it as a minimum *from* the point of breakout. This is your target length. Make allowances for a likely temporary retracement, which may revert to the original pattern.

There are *continuation* and *reversal* patterns. Continuation is when the share price continues in the same direction as before the pattern started, confirming the trend. Reversal is when a trend is changing. Unfortunately, patterns do not always work out as planned and it is not always clear whether they represent continuation or reversal.

In the examples below, I have put some key patterns in the more appropriate of the two categories, making it clear where they may have a foot in either camp. Candlestick patterns are beyond the scope of this short book, but you will find plenty of these in my book *How to Win as a Stock Market Speculator*, also published by Kogan Page.

Continuation patterns

Here are some common forms.

Flag

The flag forms in a strong trend, whether up or down, typically in less than three weeks, and technicians consider it a reliable continuation pattern. It takes the shape of a flag-like consolidation in the share price with a small price range, formed on declining volume, which is followed by a significant move. The pattern on the chart looks like a flag and its flagpole.

In an uptrend, the flag will slope downwards and, in a downtrend, upwards.

Gap

The gap takes the form of a physical break in share price movement and is often, but not always, a continuation pattern. The less frequently the gap arises, the more significant it is, particularly on a heavily traded stock. If trading volume rises with the gap, it also strengthens the message.

Technicians have identified four types of gap: common, breakaway, runaway and exhaustion.

They will usually ignore the *common* gap, which arises when trading is congested within a range due to lack of interest, a frequent situation with less liquid stocks.

The *breakaway* gap arises when the price breaks out of a range following a price reversal, and it suggests a new trend.

The *runaway* gap is rarer and signals that the trend will be continued. It is also known as the continuation or measuring gap.

The *exhaustion* gap arises when a fast move in the share price has almost reached an end. It indicates that the trend is weakening and may be a continuation or a reversal pattern.

Pennant

The pennant consists of some straight lines drawn through highs and others through lows that converge to complete a small symmetrical triangle (see under *Triangle* below). The pattern is formed on declining volume after the share price has moved up or down quickly, and usually within three weeks.

Rectangle

The rectangle is shaped as it sounds. It is a pricing range where the price swings up to a resistance line, then down to a support line until breakout. There is no rule on how many times price movements must touch the upper boundary.

The rectangle is most often a continuation pattern. This type of rectangle forms quickly, has a small price range, and is seen as more significant if it is nestling within a larger one. The rectangle can be a reversal pattern, in which case it forms more slowly and with a broader price range.

Triangle

The triangle consists of two lines that converge at an apex. One line represents resistance and the other support. The more often the share price touches these lines, the more reliable the pattern.

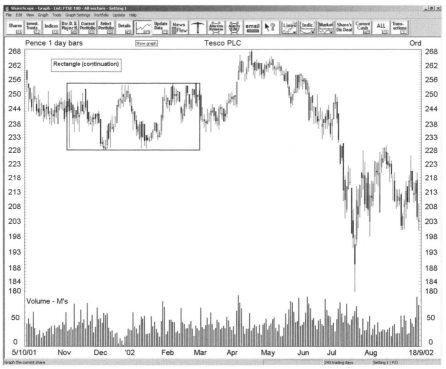

The most reliable breakouts from a triangle are believed to arise between 50 and 75 per cent towards the apex. Much earlier, the breakout is often false, meaning that the pattern is likely to continue. A symmetrical triangle has a top line that slants down and a bottom line that slants up. It may arise in an uptrend or a downtrend. If the price breaks out in the same direction as the previous trend, as is most usual, it is likely to be a continuation. If it breaks out in the opposite direction, it is likely to be a reversal.

The ascending triangle has equal highs but higher lows. In an uptrend, it is often a continuation pattern, and, in a downtrend, it is often a reversal. The descending triangle follows the same principle in reverse.

Wedge

The wedge has boundary lines that slope up or down together into an apex. If it is slanted against the trend, it indicates likely continuation. If it follows the trend, it suggests reversal. The pattern is usually completed within three months.

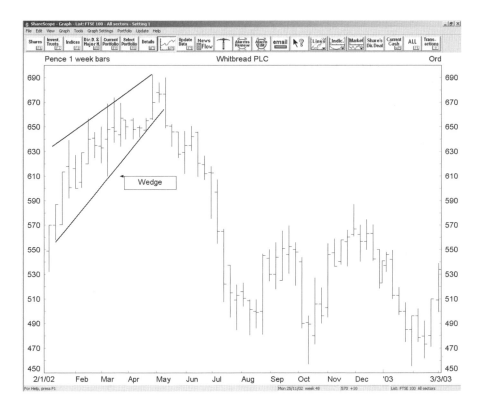

Reversal patterns

Here are some common forms.

Broadening formation

The broadening formation, known as the megaphone, is a rare bearish pattern. It arises when at least three successive peaks have each risen, accompanied by rising volume, and at least two successive troughs have fallen, accompanied by contracting volume.

The tops should be joined in one line and the bottoms in another. The two lines diverge.

Double top or bottom

The double top is a similarly rare bearish pattern and it develops usually over some months. The share price rises, falls back, then returns to its old peak, or close to it, and reverts.

The double bottom is the same in reverse, and is a bullish pattern. Some technicians consider it reliable only if trading volume rises as the second bottom is formed.

Head and shoulders

The head and shoulders is the best-known reversal pattern and is a bearish signal. The share price moves up and reverts to form the first shoulder, which is a peak in the trend. A sharp reaction will follow, and the share price dips to form a trough. It will then rise to a higher peak, which becomes the head, and will drop back again to form a second trough. The share price will rise once more, but can only form another shoulder before falling down and breaking the *support* level, which is known as the neckline.

The reverse head and shoulders is a bullish reversal signal anticipating the end of a bear market.

Saucer top or bottom

The saucer top is a rounded version of the head and shoulders or double top. It is a bearish signal that occurs in tired bull markets. It shows the share price rise, turn slowly and reverse into decline, tracing a circular motion on the chart.

Advanced theories

Fibonacci

Some theories of technical analysis are based on the Fibonacci ratios, the brainchild of Leonardo Fibonacci, a mathematician who lived in Italy 800 years ago. According to his findings, a stock market trend is likely to retrace itself by 61.8, 50 or 38.2 per cent.

The theory is rooted in Fibonacci's numerical sequence in which each number equals its two predecessors added together. The sequence reads 0, 1, 1, 2, 3, 5, 8, 13, etc. The ratio between two successive numbers in the sequence, barring the first few, is 61.8 per cent, which is known as the *golden mean*.

The Elliott Wave theory

The Fibonacci ratios helped to inspire technician Ralph Nelson Elliott into creating his famous Elliott Wave theory, which he published in 1939. According to the theory, market cycles have an impulse wave of five parts, reaching new highs, which is followed by a corrective wave of three parts. The waves interrelate according to various rules, including Fibonacci numbers.

Elliott Wave theory requires some subjective judgement, and problems arise in assessing where one wave starts and another finishes. But the framework can be made to work if the exceptions are excluded. Elliott Wave has a few fervent supporters but far more detractors.

One enthusiast of the Elliott Wave is former iconoclastic stock market trader Bob Beckman, who once said that only three people besides himself understood the theory, one of whom was dead, and another of whom had forgotten it.

Beckman's unnamed third party is likely to have been Robert Prechter, a world expert on Elliott Wave theory, who is now linked to the Socioeconomics Foundation, a think tank that has disseminated his views. The stock market reflects crowd actions and, when it is rising, so too the social mood is uplifted, and popular music and culture become more optimistic, according to Prechter. When the stock market is down, popular culture, in his experience, becomes pessimistic.

To explore such ideas further, visit www.socioeconomics.net for free access via the net to a 56-minute documentary film which presents interviews with Prechter and his supporters and with the sceptics, amidst footage of political speeches and pop culture of recent decades.

The way forward

In this module, our coverage has ranged from popular technical analysis to the more controversial aspects. In Day 10, we will turn to technical indicators.

Dynamic rules

- Traders should go with the trend for as long as it lasts.
- The resistance line is the highest point a share price reaches and the support line the lowest. The more the lines are tested, the more effective they will be.
- A trend line may be drawn against three tops or bottoms in succession and it confirms the trend.
- A trend channel covers the area between a trend line representing resistance and another representing support. If the stock is volatile, it may be traded profitably inside the channel.
- Look for continuation patterns to confirm a trend, and reversal patterns to indicate that it is changing.
- A breakout should last for as long as the depth of the pattern that precedes it.
- Fibonacci ratios offer a numerical sequence claimed to define some stock market movements. A stock market trend is considered likely to retrace itself by 61.8, 50 or 38.2 per cent.
- Elliott Wave theory explains market cycles as an impulsive wave of five parts, reaching new highs, followed by a corrective wave of three parts. The theory is controversial and requires some subjective judgement.

Secrets of technical indicators

Overview

Technical indicators confirm the message of the price charts. In this module, we will look at how they work.

Technical indicators

The technical indicator is intended to help you to improve the timing of your trades. It backs your analysis of share price trends, but is not a substitute. If indicators send out a message that contradicts the price charts, it is a warning sign.

The indicator is structured as a horizontal range on the lower part of a daily chart, and registers real-time price movement on a scale of perhaps 1–100. It is focused on price, volume or momentum. Let us look at each.

1. Price

Moving averages

Moving averages show changes in the *average* share price over a given period. They are a trend-following indicator, and so lag the share price, but can help to assess its likely future direction. Moving averages work best in a fast trend with minimum price fluctuation.

This indicator is so widely used that it is available through many free online services as well as almost any technical investment software. To understand in more detail what this indicator can do for you, it helps to know how it works, so let us delve into a little maths. Before you throw down this book in disgust, I promise you it will be very basic stuff.

To calculate a simple moving average, add up the closing prices included over the relevant number of days and divide the result by the number of prices. If you have 20 prices on the basis of one a day, you will create a 20-day moving average. This is highly sensitive because it is over a short time period, which makes it suitable for keeping track of a *short-term* investment. If you have a 200-day moving average, it is less volatile because the averages are smoothed over a longer period, which makes it suitable for keeping track of a *long-term* investment.

When the share price crosses from below to above the moving average, it could be leading the trend up and is a *buy* signal. The logic is that the shares have started outperforming the average of the recent given period. On the same basis, if the price crosses to below the moving average, this could be leading the trend down, and is a *sell* signal.

The golden cross arises when two moving averages cross over on your chart as they move upwards. It is a bullish indicator. The dead cross arises when they cross as they move downwards, and it is bearish. In either case, the indicator is more reliable if increasing trading volume backs it. The triple golden, or dead, cross involves three moving averages crossing (typically 5, 10 and 20 day), and is considered less effective.

All this is the theory and moving averages do not always stick to it, but they are another quiver to your bow. US trader Marty Schwartz has found that moving averages work better than *any* other investment timing tool at his disposal.

For the connoisseur, there are refinements. The weighted moving average gives proportionate extra weighting to more recent share prices. The exponential moving average does the same, but includes price data from outside the period of the moving average.

The moving average convergence divergence (MACD)

The moving average convergence/divergence indicator, known commonly as MACD, is a trend-following indicator that keeps you permanently in the market. The basic MACD line is formed from the difference between a 12-period and a 26-period exponential moving average of the closing price and is plotted as a *solid* line on the chart. The slow line, known as the signal line, is a nine-period exponential moving average of the MACD line and is plotted as a *dotted* line.

The MACD line and the signal line may swing either side of a zero line, and there are no overbought/oversold boundaries. Signals come late. If the MACD line crosses from beneath to above the signal line, it is the signal to take a long position. If it crosses from above to below a signal line, the signal is to take a short position.

The MACD histogram

The MACD histogram represents the difference between the MACD line and the signal line as defined above. The more the lines diverge, a process driven by the trend, the larger the histogram will become. The signals are based on how close the lines come together and so are earlier than those of the MACD indicator, which rely on the lines crossing each other.

Envelopes

The envelope, like the other indicators based on moving averages, is trend-following. It consists of a moving average of the closing price with two bands placed a given percentage either side of it. The upper band is the overbought line and the lower band the oversold.

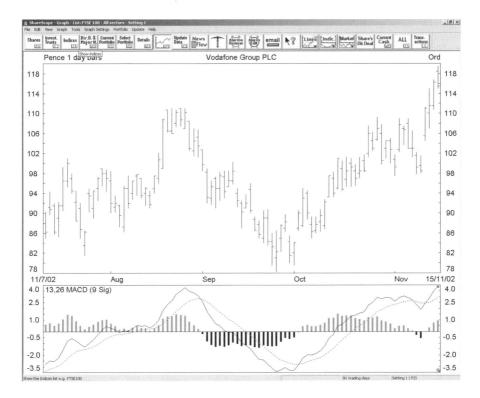

Bollinger bands are the best known member of the envelope family. John Bollinger invented the bands, based on his researches into volatility as a derivatives trader in the late 1970s. Bollinger bands are plotted at standard deviation, a volatility measure, above and below a simple moving average. The bands are based on the intermediate trend, which means a 20-day period is the most suitable.

When share prices are volatile, standard deviation becomes high and the bands bulge but, when prices are stable, it becomes low and the bands tighten. If the share price moves outside the bands, the trend is seen as likely to continue. To find out more, visit the official website at www.BollingerBands.com.

SARs

As we have seen in Chapter 4, if the share price turns against you, you are well advised to apply a stop loss. Stop and reverse points, known as SARs, are a technical solution. They are plotted as dotted lines defining a trend, and they can stop you out of either a long position or a short one.

The Parabolic indicator, created by J Wells Wilder, is a version of SARs named after the *parabola* formed by the indicator in a fast upward move. It

is sensitive to time as well as price movements, and works best when prices are moving up or down, but not sideways. It has an ingenious, built-in stop loss, which both follows the price trend and accelerates should the price have reached a new extreme. If, from this point, the trade should falter even slightly, you will be stopped out.

2. Volume

The Accumulation/Distribution line

The Accumulation/Distribution line (A/D), developed by trader Larry Williams, is a volume indicator that closely links share price and volume movements and enables you to monitor the trend. It does not provide bought and sold perimeters. The A/D line is positive if the price closes higher than at opening, and negative if it closes lower.

3. Momentum

A momentum oscillator measures both the rate of change and the direction of the share price. Traders use it for trading in ranging markets, which fluctuate between overbought and oversold lines.

They use the momentum oscillator to time their *entry* into a trending market, or their *exit*, provided the move is corroborated by a trend-following indicator. Let us look at two types: RSI and Stochastics.

RSI

The Relative Strength Index, known as RSI, shows the rate of change in the share price. Do not confuse it with *relative strength*, a concept which measures price performance against peers or the broad market (see Day 14). Some find the RSI useful, and others less so.

The Index is simple to calculate, and this is usually done over a 14-day period. The RS is the average of the *up* closes, divided by the average of the *down* closes, and it should be added to 1 to create 1+RS. Divide this figure into 100, and the result should be subtracted from 100, which gives you the RSI.

The index shows a constant range, between 0 and 100. If the RSI is 50, it is neutral. Technical analysts consider 70 overbought, and 30 oversold.

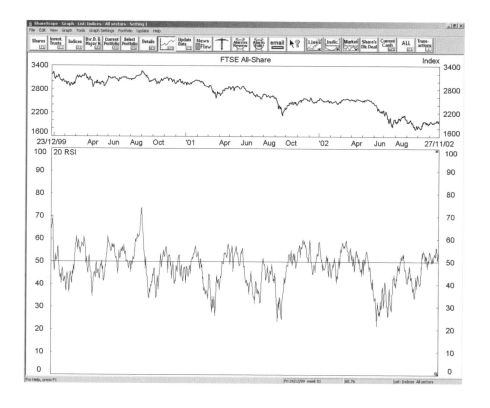

Stochastics

Stochastics, which Dr George Lane helped to develop in the 1960s, similarly shows when the market is overbought or oversold.

The oscillator shows the last closing price as a percentage of the price range over the chosen period. The solid %K line represents the share price. The dotted %D line is its three-day moving average and is considered more significant.

The two lines oscillate between 1 and 100 on a scaled chart and, as with the RSI, the overbought/oversold perimeters are usually 70–30. Traders such as Harry Schultz use Stochastics for timing their trades. When either line falls below 25 then rises above it, this is a *buy* signal, but when it overreaches 75, then slips back, this is a *sell* signal. If the moving average falls below the price line, it is often a *sell* signal.

Nowadays, the slow Stochastic is used more than the original. It excludes the %K (solid) line on the grounds that it is too sensitive. The former %D (moving average) line becomes the slowed %K line, and a slowed %D line is a moving average of this.

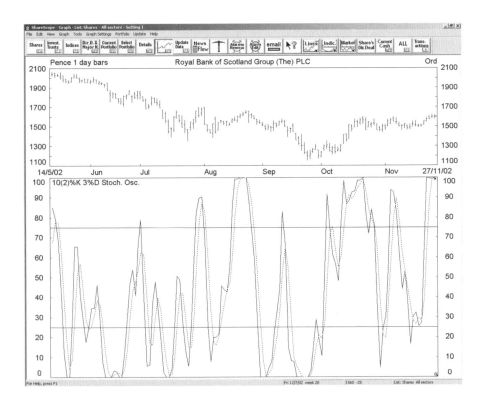

Charting facilities, tips and training

These days, you do not have to pay for online access to basic charting facilities. Try, for instance, the business pages of *Times Online* (www.timesonline. co.uk).

There are newsletters, online and in hard copy form, which offer stock tips based on the technicals. Some are jargon-intensive, and the track record may be questionable, but they help you get a grip on the charts.

If you want to learn more about technical analysis generally, you may access a short course from the website of Barclays Stockbrokers (www.stockbrokers. barclays.co.uk) without any need to register.

Let me tell you about a comprehensive course available online to UK investors. This is the basic technical analysis course, E114, from the Financial Services Institute of Australasia (www.finsia.edu.au). It is one of two legs of the Diploma in Technical Analysis awarded by the Australian Technical Analysts Association, whose website you should visit at www.ataa.com for further details.

The course notes explain important concepts such as the *trend* with a clarity and comprehensiveness that you cannot obtain from another single source. You will do a practical assignment which your tutor marks, and you will sit an exam which can be done in the UK, by arrangement with the London-based Securities & Investment Institute. Make no mistake, the course is expensive, but the quality of tutoring is superb, with queries addressed comprehensively by e-mail. As you may have guessed, I am a graduate of the programme. The course has been used as a model for some correspondence courses organized by technical analysis societies outside Australia.

The author of the course is Colin Nicholson, a self-made trader, who has his own informative website, Building Wealth Through Shares, at www.bwts. com.au.

Check out the website of the UK Society of Technical Analysts (www.sta-uk.org) which runs its own even more expensive professional courses. See the sites of the International Federation of Technical Analysts (www.ifta.org) and the US-based Market Technicians Association (www.mta.org). Read some of the books on technical analysis recommended in the appendix.

The way forward

This concludes our coverage of technical analysis. My advice to you is not to rely on it blindly. Consider fundamental factors as well.

Dynamic rules

■ Technical indicators back up share price charts but do not replace them. If an indicator contradicts the price charts, it is a warning.

■ Moving averages show changes in the average price over a given period. They lag price action but can be used to assess its future direction.

■ When the share price crosses from behind to above the moving average, it could be leading the trend up and is a buy signal. If it falls from above to below, it is a sell signal.

■ The MACD is a trend-following indicator that keeps you permanently in the market – with either a long or a short position.

■ The envelope is a moving average with an upper band, which is an overbought line, and a lower band, which denotes oversold.

■ SARs are a stop loss solution for technicians. The Parabolic indicator is an example, and it has a stop loss that accelerates once the share price has reached a new height but stops out the trader on the slightest subsequent faltering.

■ The Accumulation/Distribution line is a volume indicator that enables you to monitor the trend.

■ A momentum indicator measures the rate of change and the direction of the share price. It is for trading in ranging markets. RSI and Stochastics are examples.

Part 3

Specialist Investments

How to win in the penny share casino

Overview

In this module, we will look at types of penny stock, and how to make your selection for investment. We will look at the best ways to buy and sell, and the markets on which they are traded.

A penny for your thoughts

Penny shares can be fun but are the risky side of stock market investing. The definition of the penny share is a movable feast, but it typically sets an upper price limit. In the UK, a stock priced at less than £1.00 is widely considered a penny stock and, in the United States, the ceiling is around £3.00, encompassing stocks that were once priced at far below this level. But there are no hard and fast rules.

Liquidity is sometimes lacking in penny shares, which means they can be hard to buy and sell. Some penny stocks not listed on the London Stock Exchange Main Market have a small free float, meaning a limited number of shares in public hands. It can increase demand and send up the share price.

In reflection of the lack of liquidity, the spread (difference between buying and selling price) on a penny stock is typically wide. The share price can jump around based on only a little trading. A stock priced at 10p may rise 50 per cent on good news, whereas an old economy blue-chip stock will not. This type of gain is significant, although the spread will not enable shareholders to realize all of it. As investment guru Jim Slater has observed, elephants don't gallop but fleas can jump to over two hundred times their own height. Of course it works the other way and the penny stock can fall in value no less sharply than it may rise.

In the stock market, unlike for washing powder, price per item is not in itself linked to value and penny shares are not in themselves a bargain. But the myth about penny shares is that they are better value because the price is low.

This is a reason for the popularity of share splits, where each share is split into two or more and the price is reduced proportionately. The overall holding is in theory valued afterwards as before but the psychological appeal of more shares for your money may in itself boost the share price. The same result may apply to scrip issues (see Day 5).

The excitement generated by penny shares benefits mainly the dealers and the tipsters. Penny stocks are often poor performers that have seen better days and companies at a higher price may be of much better quality. As a penny share investor, you must be selective. Some investors pile into a favourite penny stock because they fall in love with it. The gamble occasionally pays off. But a better bet is to buy on news of corporate restructuring, new management, or a likely takeover.

More often than not, penny shares see little movement. There are some disasters, and fraud has never been far away from this market.

Markets

In the UK, the small company may be quoted on the main market of the London Stock Exchange or, if unlisted, on the Alternative Investment Market (AIM). If it is a foreign company, it may be simultaneously traded on an exchange abroad. The very small company may be PLUS-quoted, which means on the previous Ofex primary market. Let us take a more detailed look.

Main Market

There are some penny stocks traded on the London Stock Exchange Main Market. For a listing, a company normally needs a three-year track record, and 25 per cent of its shares in public hands. If it is to acquire less than 100 per cent of a target company, it must obtain shareholder approval. These rules do not apply on the AIM market (see below).

Alternative Investment Market

The Alternative Investment Market (AIM) is setting standards as a small companies market for the rest of Europe. As at March 2006, there were 1,188 domestic companies on the AIM and 220 international companies. To be quoted on the AIM avoids the higher costs and more onerous regulation of a Main Market listing. An AIM company is advised and supervised by a firm known as Nominated adviser, or Nomad, which is regulated by the London Stock Exchange.

The AIM is not a regulated market which, controversially, means that Real Estate Investment Funds, a property investment vehicle, will not be able to be quoted on it when they are introduced to the UK in early 2007.

It is a sign of strength of the market that it has substantial institutional investment. Foreign companies are increasingly quoted on the market, often by way of dual listing, which can bring risks to investors. In mid-2006, the pipeline of future market listings on the AIM was strong, although some companies had cancelled their debuts amidst stock market turbulence.

PLUS-quoted

PLUS Markets Group, an independent UK provider of equity market services, owns and operates the Ofex market for small growth companies and the PLUS trading service for shares of growth companies. By the time this book is in your hands, Ofex and the PLUS service will have merged into a single identity to be known simply as PLUS. Securities on Ofex will be called PLUS-quoted. They are traded on the PLUS trading platform alongside securities listed and traded on other exchanges, which are known as PLUS-traded.

PLUS-quoted stocks have an average market capitalization of £10–20 million, and companies look to raise up to £5 million from institutional and retail investors on the primary market, and more through secondary fundraisings. Some have raised no new cash but their shares are traded, perhaps to obtain a valuation for acquisition purposes, or to value employee share options. This *introduction* method of joining a market can enable a growing company to gain a period of experience and transparency on a public market before embarking on future capital-raising initiatives.

For investors, PLUS-quoted stocks are largely immune from the trends affecting mainstream markets. A PLUS quotation can serve as a springboard for a move to other, more senior markets. Experience of the old Ofex regime shows that you can do well if you invest in such future stars early, but many of the companies will not make a hoped-for leap. Even if they do, not every such company will necessarily sustain the higher listing. Some find it hard to adjust to the resulting sudden increase in their shareholder base and greater liquidity, with share price fluctuations arising.

For more details, visit the PLUS Markets Group website (www. plusmarketsgroup.com). Also see the site of unquoted.co.uk (www.unquoted. co.uk) for access to, among other things, useful bulletin boards.

Markets abroad

By June 2006, when the AIM had reached its 11th anniversary, some rival small company markets were operating in continental Europe.

In May 2005, Euronext, the cross-border exchange, launched its junior market, Alternext, which offers access to four countries. In October 2005, Deutsche Börse launched its junior market Entry Standard, which has 32 companies in sectors ranging from renewable energy to nano technology and financial services. Unlike on the AIM, companies on this market must have a fully vetted prospectus and there are no tax concessions.

In the United States, Nasdaq (www.nasdaq.com) has some small companies and it offers a more heavily regulated alternative to the AIM. The market is fully electronic, which makes it liquid and transparent.

Unless you know what you are doing, avoid US over-the-counter (OTC) stocks, some of which are quoted on the US-based Pink Sheets (www.pinksheets.com). The OTC issuers do not have to register with the Securities & Exchange Commission, the US regulator. Many OTC securities are relatively illiquid, and fraud and manipulation in this market are commonplace.

Types of penny share

Penny shares may be loosely categorized as growth, recovery, shell and cyclical. There is some overlap.

Growth

Many growth companies will be high-tech, and tangible assets may be thin on the ground. You should value small growth companies using discounted cash flow (DCF) analysis and, if they have earnings, the P/E ratio or PEG and, if not, perhaps the price/sales ratio (see Day 7). Do not expect dividends.

Since the bubble of soaring prices of internet stocks burst in March 2000, some of the revenue-based valuation methods (see Day 1) have all but disappeared. Real option pricing puts a value on the company's flexibility to take appropriate actions in a variety of scenarios and, as a valuation method, it survived the dot com fallout. It is only as good as the information fed into its models.

Biotechnology companies

Biotechnology companies are viewed as a high-risk, high-reward alternative to pharmaceuticals. The UK has 500 biotechnology companies and only a fraction of the products under consideration gets from discovery to marketing approval. The success rate improves once products have cleared early hurdles. Pharmaceutical companies may help to fund the product trials of their smaller cousins.

The most usual way to value biotechnology companies is through discounted cashflow analysis (see Day 7), or using the price/research ratio (share price divided by Research and Development per share). In addition, compare cash burn, which is cash spent, with cash held, and watch how close key products are to completion.

If a main product fails, the share price is likely to plunge. In 1996, British Biotech's shares were 300p but they plummeted after the company's Marimistat cancer drug turned out to be ineffective. By June 2000, the share price was 19.25p.

The investor risk is reduced if the company has a pipeline of at least several products, including some with a large market, although this also increases the competition, as happened in HIV and cancer therapies.

For developments in the sector, visit the US sites Biospace.com (www. biospace.com) and Recap.com (www.recap.com).

Recovery

Recovery stocks are former stock market darlings that fell out of favour. The company will have survived only because it restructured its business, perhaps lopping off unprofitable divisions or making a synergistic acquisition.

There is some hope that recovery stocks may return to glory and investor sentiment can be strong. The share price may double in value within a week, or in a few months, but on setbacks it may fall as hard. Compare the current price with the high and low over the past 12 months. A share may not repeat the old price patterns, but such data still tells you something.

Look for a trading prompt. An upgrade in analysts' consensus forecasts or directors' buying can be a green light. A new broom as chief executive can work wonders. But some companies have problems that are not resolvable by direct action, and you should steer clear.

Shell

A shell company is a quoted company that does not trade. It may be dirty or clean. A dirty shell is an ex-operating business. It may have transferred its business to a subsidiary or to a parent, and be a form of recovery situation (see above). A clean shell is not so encumbered and can be preferable from an investment perspective. It will have been formed to seek acquisitions. The usual way is through a reverse takeover, where the company taken over seizes control.

To reverse into a shell can be a cheap and convenient way for an unquoted company with a limited track record to obtain a Main Market or AIM quotation. If it happens, the shares will be suspended for about six weeks, and will then be quoted again, perhaps at a higher price.

The garden is not always so rosy. Clean shells have been known to sell shares to investors on acquisition plans that have come to nothing. You may prefer to wait until a deal has been announced *before* you invest your money.

New disclosure rules for AIM stocks have made it less risky to invest in shells. If an investing company was admitted to the AIM before 1 April 2005 and raised less than £3 million at admission, it had until 1 April 2006 either to make an acquisition through a reverse takeover or to satisfy the London Stock Exchange it had carried out its investing strategy. Companies that failed the criteria were suspended from the AIM with an ultimate threat of removal from the market.

The minimum £3 million of investment in shells means that institutional investors are involved enough to provide essential stops and checks, according to the London Stock Exchange. The dirty shells must obtain shareholder agreement at annual general meetings to extend their lifespan by 12 months. A company that fails to obtain this agreement will be dissolved.

Cyclical

Cyclical stocks rise and fall with the business cycle. The businesses include, among others, house-building, construction, steel, car manufacturing and distribution, and resources. You should buy near the bottom of the cycle, when, for example, a good house builder is buying land cheap and selling it at high margins before competition starts muscling in.

The better known the company, the stronger its backing and the more easily it can exploit the bottom of the cycle. The less well-known companies often have bigger growth potential, but the investment risk is higher. Resource companies are exposed to the crude oil price, which is subject to political and economic risk. A majority of AIM companies are in the sector. Unlike the oil majors such as BP and Shell, the tiddlers do not have downstream activities such as refining and petrol stations to generate income if the price of crude oil declines.

Invest in cyclical survivors. If turnover has stayed steady in a recession, it is a good sign and some decline in profits may easily be reversible, perhaps through a cost-cutting programme. In a property company, asset backing per share is ideally higher than the share price. This provides support in lean times and, if the company is wound up, the liquidator will pay shareholders in proportion to the company's assets. It also attracts predators.

Stock selection

Valuation and industry trends

Financial ratios count for less in penny stocks than in larger ones, not least because the underlying company is less likely to have earnings or tangible assets. The share price can soar on rumours but can just as quickly drop back if, as is very likely, they prove unfounded. Some investors buy profitably for the short term.

Creative accounting is more difficult under today's reporting standards than in the past but it is still worth watching for it on the financial statements. Check that annual depreciation (see Day 7) is not so small that it barely hits the profit & loss account. Be wary if an item that would normally be an expense in the profit & loss account is instead capitalized on the balance sheet.

Try to predict rather than follow industry trends. Takeover rumours or corporate restructuring may give a fillip to the share price.

Management

Assess the management of the companies in which you are considering investing. Look for leadership and technical expertise, which are often not combined in the same people. For example, Charles Muirhead, a 25-year-old technology genius, employed experienced management to run Orchestream, his software company that was listed on the London Stock Exchange in July 2000.

A change in management can send the share price soaring in anticipation of a positive earnings surprise. You can gain an inkling of pending staff changes by watching the company's recruitment advertising in trade or national press.

Buying and selling techniques

Market maker tactics

A market maker in penny shares is likely to deal only in small quantities at the price it quotes. If you try to buy or sell more, the firm is likely to ratchet the price up or down.

In a rising stock market, the market maker needs to find sellers, so *shakes the tree* and marks the share price down sharply, causing some shareholders to sell in panic. The market maker then raises the price again, and the sellers repurchase the stock. When this rise is temporary, it is known as a *dead cat bounce*.

Spread your risk

Spread your risk by investing in several penny stocks rather than just one. The combined total should amount to no more than 10–15 per cent of your equities portfolio. Of course, not all your investments should be equities.

Dealers

One way to buy penny shares is through a dedicated dealer. It is dangerous because the firm may not give you impartial advice, even if it claims to, and it may target you with some kind of share ramp. The risk arises because the dealer acts as principal, which means it buys shares in bulk, and sells them on to clients at a higher price. It is acting in its own interest, and this may not also be years.

The dealer's offer price may sometimes be below the open market price, but this does not in itself mean a bargain. See Day 19 for details of the pump-and-dump, a favourite of some penny share dealers.

Tax advantages

There are tax advantages for investors in *unlisted* small companies, including PLUS-quoted and AIM, but, as in any investing, the golden rule is that you should consider the investment case first. If you lose every penny of your investment, tax relief will be scant compensation.

In the next few paragraphs, I will explain the main tax options. See also the website of HM Revenue & Customs (www.hmrc.gov.uk).

The Enterprise Investment Scheme

Under the Enterprise Investment scheme (EIS), some unlisted small companies offer you 20 per cent income tax relief for up to £400,000 a year (2006–7) invested in new ordinary shares, and capital gains tax exemption. You can defer unlimited capital gains tax arising from disposal of other assets by reinvesting your gains in EIS companies. This tax is deferred until the shares are sold. You may obtain income tax relief by way of election for capital losses suffered.

To qualify for the tax reliefs on EIS shares, you must hold them and meet the qualifying conditions for three years. You must be unconnected with the company in which you plan to invest, and it must be UK-based, unquoted, and carrying on a qualifying business, or intended to do so. Barred activities include financing, law, property investment, hotels, gardening and farming.

Inheritance tax exemption

Once you have held unquoted shares for two years, they are exempt from inheritance tax (see Day 5).

The way forward

Penny shares are exciting, but are often little more than gambling. If you want to dabble, at least do your own research and do not rely entirely on somebody else's tip.

Dynamic rules

- Penny shares can lack liquidity. They have wide spreads and the price may move sharply on only a little trading.
- The Alternative Investment Market is less regulated than the Main Market, and has many companies with foreign assets.
- PLUS-quoted stocks are small and unlisted. They are largely immune from trends affecting mainstream markets.
- Unless you know what you are doing, avoid the high-risk US OTC market.
- Wait until a newish shell company has announced a deal before you invest in it.
- Recovery stocks may become takeover targets. If you invest in these early enough, you can sometimes make good money.
- Buy cyclical stocks near the bottom of the cycle and favour survivors.
- Investors may feel that penny stocks offer more for their money because the share price is low. It is an illusion, but a share split or scrip issue provides a psychological boost that can lead to a price rise.
- Creative accounting still goes on. Be wary if depreciation is too small or an item normally expensed is capitalized on the balance sheet.
- Look for leadership and technical expertise in the management, but not necessarily in the same person.
- Avoid the dedicated penny share dealers because they act as principals and may not give you impartial advice.
- Never invest in unquoted companies only for the tax perk.

Pooled investment made easy

Overview

In this module we will focus on pooled investments, which you can buy and sell online. We will concentrate mainly on investment funds and investment trusts.

Investment funds – the lazy person's way

People invest in funds when they don't have the time, energy or knowledge to invest directly in equities. It is the lazy man's way. You have to put a lot of work into choosing the right investment fund. But once you have done so, you leave the donkey work of selecting and monitoring stocks to the fund manager.

You need to watch the fund's overall performance. Even the top funds have ups and downs, and you should not panic at fluctuations. But if, in the longer term, the fund stops performing well against its peers or, indeed, in absolute terms, or seems likely to do so, be ready to jump ship.

If you buy your investment fund online, using your stockbroker or fund supermarket, there may be a rebate on a substantial part of the initial charges, and sometimes of annual management charges, provided in the form of extra units. But you will receive no specific investment advice.

Should you buy through a traditional financial adviser, you will pay commission but will receive advice. The adviser today is not likely to have detailed knowledge of all the funds on offer, which are well over 25,000.

The advisory role is moving away from product selection and more towards provision of an overall solution for the client's needs.

Unit trusts or OEICs

Investment funds can be unit trusts, or the more modern open-ended investment trusts, known as OEICs. The two have technical distinctions but they serve the same purpose in giving investors access to a managed fund with a variety of assets, so diversifying risk and reducing dealing costs. Investment funds are open-ended, meaning that the fund can create or redeem as many further units for a unit trust, or shares for an OEIC, as are required to meet investor demand.

The unit trust has two prices: that at which you buy, the *offer* price, and that at which you sell, the *bid* price. The difference is the spread, which incorporates initial charges and dealing costs. The OEIC has a single price, linked directly to the value of the fund's investments.

Funds enable you to gain a diversified portfolio managed on your behalf, and your investment can be small. You can reduce the exposure to market volatility by drip-feeding your money into the fund monthly, which means that the average unit price paid is linked to the average price of the stock over the time period of your investment. It means you will not have lost from buying disproportionately when the market was high, but nor will you have gained from doing so when the market was low.

Performance surveys confirm that at least 75 per cent of funds fail to beat the market average once all charges are taken into account. To avoid this trap, go for a tracker fund.

Tracker fund

This type of fund aims only to replicate the market by tracking a popular market index such as the FTSE-100. The tracker fund tends to have low charges and has produced a higher overall return than the majority of actively managed funds once charges are taken into account.

Actively managed fund

In a falling market, actively managed funds may be a better bet. Unlike the tracker, they can reduce exposure to equities and hold cash until conditions improve, but many prefer to stay fully invested.

There are a few actively managed funds that seem to outperform regularly and they are often your best bet, but there can never be certainty.

If the fund manager leaves his or her post, it can be a catalyst for a change in performance.

In the past, funds have aimed to outperform peers or the market, but investors have not always been satisfied. If a fund is down 10 per cent, it will have made a loss even if it outperformed the market. The trend now is moving from relative to absolute performance targeting.

To choose a managed fund in which to invest, you will need to do your research and compare funds on past performance. I particularly recommend that you visit Trustnet at www.trustnet.co.uk and Morningstar UK at www. morningstar.co.uk. Interactive Investor (www.iii.co.uk) has good impartial advice on its site on how to select funds.

The investment fund industry mantra, driven by regulatory requirements, is that past performance is no guide to the future. Industry advisers suggest it is, nonetheless, often the best one we have.

As a rough guide, look for funds that have been in the top quartile of the sector by performance over the past five years. Be warned that the top performing fund in any given year has often put in a mediocre performance the following year.

You should assess the fund's charges because they will reduce your returns. There is an initial charge, which includes the commission paid to the adviser or broker who sold you the fund. In the absence of a discount, this is up to 6 per cent of your money invested. In a unit trust, the initial charge is accounted for by most of the bid–offer spread. The OEIC itemizes the initial charge separately on the transaction statement.

In addition, an annual management fee, which is a percentage of the value of the investor's holding in the year, and other fees are payable.

The best way to compare charges on investment funds is through the total expense ratio, which shows the full charges caused by all annual operating costs as a proportion of the fund's average assets. This is more comprehensive than the widely quoted management charge. Some online stockbrokers and fund data services provide this ratio.

Multi-manager funds

The multi-manager fund is worth considering because it is well diversified and the performance can be excellent. It comes in two main types. The first is the fund of funds, where a manager invests in a variety of other investment funds. The second and cheaper type is a manager-of-managers scheme, where various fund managers are each given part of the fund to invest in the stock market.

Buying investment funds

Fund supermarkets

The fund supermarket offers an enticing range of discounted funds online, complete with self-selection tools and data for comparing profiles and performance. It can be an Aladdin's cave for the independent fund investor.

The fund supermarket model came to the UK in 2000 after it had operated for some years in the United States. As an example of what it can offer, visit Fidelity Funds Network at www.fundsnetwork.co.uk.

Online stockbrokers

Some online stockbrokers sell funds online and provide useful comparative statistics and profiles. Hargreaves Lansdown (www.hargreaveslansdown.co.uk) is a good first port of call because it displays information about selected funds exceptionally clearly.

Investment trusts

The investment trust is often compared with an investment fund. It is also a pooled investment but it is differently structured and is less publicized. The investment trust is a quoted company which invests in companies.

Unlike an investment fund, it is a closed-ended fund, which means it has a fixed number of shares in issue at any one time. For every buyer of an investment trust share, there must be a seller, and the share price will fluctuate.

Investment trusts are riskier than their open-ended cousins because they are usually geared, meaning they borrow cash, and the share price trades at a varying discount (or less often, a premium) to net asset value. They have an adventurous image and the annual management charge tends to be lower than on investment funds. They have in common with the funds that they often fail to beat the market average.

Venture capital trusts (VCTs)

Venture capital trusts (VCTs) are quoted companies that invest in small growth companies. You can buy them directly or through your stockbroker or financial adviser. The shares are little traded and the spread tends to be wide.

The VCT must choose its investments within three years and hold at least 70 per cent of them in qualifying, unquoted UK companies trading in the UK. In 2005, sales of VCTs to investors reached a record £507 million. The annual charges are higher than on a conventional investment trust.

The VCT will plan to exit from a company in which it has invested through either a stock market listing or a takeover. Should a company achieve a London Stock Exchange listing, it may stay a VCT investment for five years. If the VCT is taken over, shareholders will take a cut of the price paid.

In the 2006 Budget, Chancellor Gordon Brown introduced major changes for VCTs effective from 6 April. The 40 per cent income tax relief available on VCT subscription was reduced to 30 per cent, and the most money VCT managers could invest in individual companies was cut from £15 million to £7 million.

The new environment has made VCTs riskier and the returns lower, according to critics. In 2005, the Financial Services Authority had identified VCTs as an area of potential risk to consumers.

Exchange-traded funds

Structurally an exchange-traded fund (ETF) is a derivative that combines elements of both an investment fund and an investment trust. You can buy the ETF on margin and there are no setup charges. It trades like ordinary shares on the London Stock Exchange, and each unit tracks an index or sector. Like an investment fund, the ETF is open-ended, which means it can issue more units to meet demand. ETFs are increasingly used by hedge funds, an unregulated type of pooled investment fund that uses a variety of trading strategies in the quest for highest absolute returns.

Your pension

You can include investment funds or trusts, or other investments in your pension, which is a tax-efficient wrapper, and this can often be organized through your broker. If you start a self-invested personal pension (SIPP), you will be able to choose your own investments from a wide universe, including investment funds and shares.

The way forward

Investment funds or investment trusts are useful if you do not have much money to invest but want a diversified portfolio. They are suitable for less experienced investors because they do not require stock-picking or asset allocation skills. But you must put in time and effort in choosing your fund. Once you have it, you should keep an eye on its performance and strategic direction.

Dynamic rules

- Investment funds enable you to achieve diversification for a small investment.
- Most investment funds fail to beat the market average after all charges are taken into account.
- The best way to compare charges on any investment fund is to use the total expenses ratio.
- The cheapest type of investment fund is the tracker fund.
- Multi-manager funds offer excellent diversification.
- Investment trusts are riskier than investment funds because they are geared and the share price trades at a varying discount to net asset value.

How to make a killing on new issues

Overview

In this module, we will look at new equity issues and how you can profit from them. We will look at how they are priced and the process of bringing them to the market, including timing.

How a new issue works

A new issue of shares takes place when a company is floated on the stock market. Subsequently, the company's shares are traded on what is known as the secondary market.

Pricing

Even if you are investing in a *good* company at issue, this is not enough in itself for you to make a profit. The price must be right.

The key point is that a new issue of shares is priced according to *demand*. In a bull market, where institutional investors are competing for shares in every hot new issue almost regardless of its quality, the price can be much higher than the company's fundamental value. But it is the best time to buy and sell new issues at a profit. In a bear market the price can be lower, which may prove a bargain in the medium or long term, but not necessarily.

The syndicate

The investment bank or broker organizing the deal is known as book runner and sometimes global coordinator. It sets the price and manages distribution of the shares. The job of book runner is sought after, and the fees are often high. Banks compete for this role by making formal presentations to the issuing company. It is quaintly termed a *beauty parade*.

In a large new issue of shares, two banks are often appointed as joint global coordinators and joint book runners. The book runner will probably have a track record of floating similar companies and a good understanding of the business.

The fees charged are a factor in winning the business but are rarely the priority. Most IPOs and secondary placings are handled by banks that have a corporate relationship with the issuing company, according to research from investment bankers.

The bank that wins the mandate may have expertise in the company's sector or a special relationship with its country of origin. But any conflict of interests will rule out an appointment.

The chosen book runner appoints a syndicate of banks to help place stock with institutions and private clients, and announces an overall fee structure. In the syndicate there may be one local bank that typically handles private clients (known as retail). The other banks will probably sell mainly to institutions, but there is no fixed rule. Every bank in the syndicate is given a prestigious title such as co-lead manager or co-manager.

Pre-marketing

Next comes the pre-marketing phase of the deal, where banks meet with institutional investors to assess demand for the shares. The book runner accordingly sets an indicative price range to provide perimeters within which the new issue will be priced. The bank often makes this range public.

Valuations

Once they know the price range, analysts can put forward a valuation on the company to be listed, based on respective issue prices at the lower, mid and upper end of the range. Financial journalists may report analysts' valuations and provide critical comment. Nothing is definitive until the deal is actually priced, owing to the following three factors:

▓ The range might be very wide, which makes prospective valuations meaningless.

■ The range is not set in stone. Banks involved in the flotation may occasionally move it up or down to meet changing demand, particularly in a strong bull market or when markets are volatile.

■ The deal may be postponed or cancelled. This is more likely if the market has slid severely between the time the range was set and the deal was priced, and if the issuing company is a young, not well-known one.

In practice

In June 2006, the certainties became apparent after global stock markets had declined sharply although, as it turned out, temporarily, in value. Standard Life, the mutual life insurer, was one company that cut the price range on its flotation, and many planned share issues were cancelled.

Demand creation

The price range in any deal plays a crucial role in attracting institutional investor demand for the shares. If the book runner values an issue low enough in setting the range and, ultimately, the price, it encourages over-subscription.

In a bull market, over-subscription may happen anyway because institutional investors that want stock will always apply for more than they expect to receive. Demand for new equity issuance is created in part through controlled release of news to the media.

This is the task of the PR agencies. Skilful PR can mitigate the damage of adverse news but will not necessarily remove it. There are always a few maverick journalists who refuse to accept the company's official line. For more on PR and press shenanigans, see Day 18.

Book build

Following the pre-marketing of a deal and the setting of a price range, the banks start to build up the book of demand for the new issue. In a road-show lasting two or three weeks, they present the company to institutional investors, either in groups or, more effectively, in *one-to-ones*. The road-show can extend across continental Europe and the United States as well as the UK, and may be supplemented by video-conferencing for countries not visited. The road-show demands time from the company's chief executive, finance director and head of investor relations, which takes them away from running the business.

Institutional interest is fickle and can wane on adverse company, sector or market conditions. Investors tend to hold off their orders for shares until the last minute. The book runner and syndicate put up with all this uncertainty because the business, if it goes ahead, is usually highly lucrative.

Clients

Syndicate bankers normally give priority of allocation to institutional clients, but welcome the involvement of private investors because they help to swell the order book.

Private investors make a significant contribution to holding up the company's share price in secondary market trading because they are less inclined to sell out quickly. If they are involved, banks can price the new issue higher.

Research before committing your cash

Before you subscribe, find out about the issuing company. Read the prospectus and use the following resources.

Analysts

The book runner will have its own research on a stock to be launched on the market, but assess it cautiously. As a result of the corporate link, the analysts will probably have a superior grasp of the company's business, but will also have good reason to feel sympathetic towards it.

Some years ago, a leading syndicate banker confided in me that, in bull markets, he and his colleagues dictated what the analysts wrote. Regulations have done much to end these *glory* days. Even so, bear in mind that investment banking remains highly lucrative for the firm that employs the analyst.

Make a point of listening to analysts in leading City banks that are uninvolved in the deal. Of course, these analysts too have their angle and may not always put what they think in their written reports for fear of offending companies. Analysts can also be wrong.

Press

Financial journalists are less knowledgeable than analysts, but are not similarly juggling commercial interests. They have access to experts and an ear to the ground. Everybody makes mistakes but if the *journos* collectively agree that a deal is over- or under-priced, they are probably right.

National newspapers and consumer finance websites are a useful source of news and gossip. If the new issues bug bits hard, read *Financial News*, a gossipy weekly trade magazine that has excellent coverage of capital markets. For the online version, visit www.efinancialnews.com.

Syndicate desk

If you ring the syndicate desk of the book runner to a new issue, you may find a friendly person who will discuss the deal, but don't rely on it. If a banker does let his or her tongue wag, read between the lines. I have known bankers wax lyrical about a book build, and how major institutions have already placed big orders – then, hours later, the deal is pulled, owing to lack of demand.

The grey market

Another way to monitor sentiment about a pending new issue is to check the grey market price. This is the value that the spread betting firms (see Day 16) put on the shares before the deal is priced. It applies only to a few, high-profile share issues.

When publicized in the press, the grey market price can sometimes have a disproportionate influence on institutional and other investor sentiment. It is based on, at most, a few hundred bets.

Be warned. Grey market prices are unscientifically assessed and have proved an unreliable predictor of pricing. In some share issues, the grey market price has been high, but the stock has been priced lower and, subsequently, has fallen further.

How to apply successfully for new issues

Big names

When banks or brokers promote a new issue, it does not in itself mean that the issuer is a good company, or on offer at a good price. The banks should ensure high standards of process, including disclosure, but they earn their fees from a flotation regardless of how well the shares later perform.

Venture capitalist backing gives a fillip to capital markets but do not assume that you will benefit. A deal will have been planned to give the VC a profitable exit from its stake, perhaps 40 per cent of the equity. As a small investor, you are unlikely to have the same opportunity.

Markets

If you invest in companies floating on the Main Market of the London Stock Exchange, you will benefit from more rigorous standards than on other UK markets. The AIM offers some great opportunities if you can stomach the risks of a non-regulated market. PLUS-quoted stocks have competing market makers, which provide the market with liquidity. For more about these two junior markets, see Day 11.

Practical steps

To subscribe to a new issue, you can often apply through your broker, or a website that specializes in new issues. For some internet company flotations, your application must go through the issuing company's own site.

As an online applicant, you will download a form, which you must complete and send with your cheque to the book runner of the deal by *snail mail* because the signature must be original. Note that multiple applications are easily discovered and can lead to prosecution.

Be selective. It is easy to be seduced by glowing online write-ups of pending new issues, and the technology can make the application process seem no more complicated than pressing a few keys on your computer. It is the quality of the company, its valuation, and sector and market conditions that count, and they will not always all be good.

I should mention that online subscription to a popular deal can have technical complications. Once I registered for the share offering of a Scandinavian internet company and the prerequisite downloading of the prospectus proved almost impossible. New issue subscribers have reported similar experiences elsewhere.

Upon issue

Get flipping mad

In a bull market, a share issue, even when overpriced, will typically reach a small premium to the issue price, perhaps 10–15 per cent, in early secondary market trading. This can generate further demand, particularly when the free float is small, which limits the proportion of shares publicly available. But if the share price is higher than the fundamentals justify, there will later be a rebalancing.

If you subscribe to the issue, it is often best to make hay while the sun shines and to *flip* or *stag* the shares, which is to sell them for a quick profit in the first few days of trading.

The book runner will try to discourage flipping because a mass exodus from a new issue could send the share price into free fall. It could make the deal appear to have been overpriced, which brings adverse publicity, and the bank may be forced to support the share price, a process known as stabilization.

The book runner will not dare to discourage the large institutional investors from flipping the stock because it will need their participation in future share offerings. It may take a more cavalier attitude to private investors.

In the July 2000 flotation of Carphone Warehouse, the mobile telephone retailer, private investors received priority allocation only if they would hold the shares for three months. The same pressure was not put on institutional investors.

Buy recently issued stock in the secondary market

If you are interested in a new issue and it is likely to be overpriced, wait until the deal has taken place. If the shares are worth buying, they should still be so in the secondary market. Should the share price then be too high, you can wait until it has declined before you commit your money.

The way forward

Online technology has made new issues more accessible to the private investor but they are still a game for institutional investors. If you plan on getting involved, be selective over what you buy and when, and do not hold back from selling.

Dynamic rules

- ■ It is best to buy and sell new issues in a bull market.
- ■ New issues are priced according to demand and not necessarily with reference to fundamental value. It can be outside the indicative range.
- ■ Institutional investors usually receive priority allocation of shares in a new issue.
- ■ It is often best to flip new issues, which is to sell the shares allocated to you in early secondary market trading.
- ■ If the issue price seems too high, put off your buying decision until the stock is trading in the secondary market.
- ■ In researching a new issue, consult at least analysts' output and the press. Watch the grey market price if there is one because it can have a disproportionate effect on investors.

- To play safe, go for new issues on the Main Market of the London Stock Exchange rather than the junior markets or abroad.
- Do not assume that you will profit from a new issue simply because it is backed by top-name banks or venture capitalists.

Part 4

Trading and Derivatives

How to win as a share trader

Overview

In this module we will start by looking at how you prepare to become a trader, including the risks, the reasons for success and failure, and different categories of trading. We will see how to develop your own trading system and protect your capital. We will consider how to place your order, including limit and market orders, and money management.

Preparing to trade

A high-risk business

As a share trader you can make – or lose – thousands of pounds in seconds. It is not always so extreme, and sometimes may be more so. You can take a long position to gain from rising markets or a short position to gain from the fallers. You can hedge your main position.

On a day-to-day basis, stock prices do not necessarily gravitate towards book value, as they do over time. As a trader, you cannot rely on fundamentals. The share price is driven by mass buying and selling, largely based on sentiment. On this basis, Gerald M Loeb, a great US trader of the early 20th century, said that accountants made bad traders and psychologists good ones.

How far you succeed depends more on you than on market conditions. If you apply good money management (covered later in this module), you can win, even if you have entered more losing than winning trades. To run your winners and cut your losses is truly a secret of success.

It is on the early learning curve that you are most likely to lose money. Your early efforts will also give you the opportunity to assess whether the trading game is right for you. You will risk losing not just your money but, with it, some friends, status and perhaps your self-respect.

See the risks as temporary because, if your approach is right, you will later gain any losses back and much more. In his classic poem *If*, Rudyard Kipling wrote:

> If you can make one heap of all your winnings
> And risk it on one turn of pitch-and-toss
> And lose, and start again at your beginnings
> And never breathe a word about your loss
> Yours is the Earth and everything that's in it
> And – which is more – you'll be a Man, my son!

If you have the stomach for share trading, you will enjoy the ride. If you are a little scared, that is good, as it can make you be more careful. Stuart Watson, who has an outstanding record of trading equities through his US-based firm Reindeer Capital, believes that *anyone* can do the job of trading, and that you do not have to be born to it. Of course, you need to understand the basics.

Position yourself in the market

Your trading base

Most individual share traders work from home. It is ideal for some, and it means they can get on with other things once the markets are too choppy for trading. But home trading can bring distractions. It is a lonely business, even with access to web-based trading communities, and not everybody has what it takes.

If you are trading from home, set up a dedicated office, with telephone, computer and any other screens. You should have easy access to newspapers, company reports and accounts, research and similar. This is your workplace.

Frequent traders need access to streaming share prices and Level II information. Not all will make the investment.

Categories of share trading

Share trading breaks down into three broad categories: day, swing and position trading.

- As a day trader, you close out your position every day, and so avoid the risk of holding shares overnight. You will make your profits from intraday market volatility.
- As a swing trader, you hold shares for between two and five days, which gives more time for success, and for failure.
- As a position trader, you hold shares for between one and two months, which gives you even more flexibility.

Some traders operate in more than one of these categories simultaneously. It works well, but only as part of a deliberate strategy.

General trading principles

Develop your own system

To trade successfully, you will need your own trading system. The techniques described in this module and in the rest of this book are your box of tricks, but you should select from them to build it. Once you have your system in place, fine-tune it. Do not abandon it to suit particular trading circumstances, or it will not function as a system at all.

What works for one trader may not for another. Some trade within hours, others within weeks, days or hours. Some study fundamentals, and others – although they are fewer than the software promoters would have you believe – follow the charts. Many follow news flow, instinct and the crowd, or jump on the bandwagon of guru-led activity or director trades.

Use limit orders

On Day 3, I said I would tell you today why you should use limit orders, so here we go. When you buy shares, you can place a *market* order, which means that you will buy at the market price, but it can change rapidly, and you may find yourself paying more than you had expected.

If you instead set a *limit* order, you will control what you pay. If the order is not fulfilled at the price that you have specified, it is cancelled. Hey, you are in charge. This is the route that the professional traders take.

When you sell shares, you could also place a *sell limit* order, so specifying the lowest price that you will accept for your shares. I advise against it. I have known traders place one sell limit order after another, but they do not sell because the share price keeps falling too fast to enable the successive limits to be applied.

As a seller, place a *market* order. The deal will be completed faster, even if the price is not always ideal. The benefit of this is to free up your capital to trade elsewhere without delay.

Self-discipline and proportion

When a stock has risen to a comfortable profit level, you will want to hold on to the shares to make more money. Conversely, when a share is falling, you will also want to hold on in the hope of a reversal. In both cases, you should usually do the opposite.

Some traders invest a very high proportion of their available capital on one trade. This is a mistake because even the most likely winning trade can go wrong. As a trader, do not make the mistake of getting attached to the stock. It should be nothing to you except an instrument for trading.

You should not buy so many stocks that you cannot keep an eye on them properly. This is a practical issue, separate from the investment case surrounding diversification. The great US trader Jesse Livermore would buy only leading stocks in leading industries. If these stocks should weaken, it was a sign that other stocks could follow suit. On this basis he called the great stock market crash of 1929.

Protect your trading capital

Trade only with capital you can afford to lose. Perhaps, as trading guru Toni Turner has recommended online, traders should shout to themselves throughout the trading day: 'Protect my principal.' The message has added resonance once you are approaching the heady heights of retirement age. Do not then trade with your life savings. As renowned US trader Ed Seycota has said, 'There are old traders and there are bold traders, but there are very few old, bold traders.'

Review your mistakes

Expect to lose money sometimes as a trader. In the November 1997 issue of *Technically Speaking*, the newsletter of the Market Technicians Association, US trading guru Dr Van K Sharp wrote an article: 'Why it's so difficult for most people to make money on the market'. He argued: 'Most of us grew up exposed to an educational system that brainwashes us with the idea that you have to get

94%–95% correct to be excellent. … Mistakes are severely punished in the school system by ridicule and poor grades, yet it is only through mistakes that human beings learn.'

Let us keep this in perspective. As trader Robert P Rotella said in *The Elements of Successful Trading* (New York Institute of Finance): 'Losing money when you begin trading is the price paid in learning how to trade and enter the business. But do not be misled into thinking the higher the tuition paid, the better the education.'

The great traders have always reviewed their losing trades, and tried to learn where they went wrong. Gerald Loeb would write down the reasons for making a trade before he entered it, and it made his retrospective analysis easier.

Be professional

Some traders treat share trading more like a hobby than a job but they are competing against professionals. As a trader you need to commit your time and energy to watching the markets properly, and applying proven rules. US trader Jesse Livermore considered stock speculation a full-time job that required a full-time focus. Bernard Baruch, another trader of genius, took a similar view.

Money management

Capital commitment

Money management is about how much of your capital you should speculate on a given trade, and when. Here is your safeguard against being wiped out too quickly by oversized trade. Good money management does not guarantee success but you will not get very far without it.

In 1987, US trader Larry Williams turned US~$10,000 into US~$1.1 million within 12 months and he attributed his success to money management. Williams bought more contracts when he had plenty of cash and less when he did not, which sounds simple enough but, like other aspects of money management, it requires self-discipline.

The first rule of money management is to decide how much capital you will commit to trading. If you are on the cautious side, you could start with 10 per cent of your savings. If your savings are £100,000, this would be £10,000. If your savings are much smaller, you could use a higher percentage, although it increases the risk.

To preserve your trading capital is your priority and you should not trade with too much of it at once. If your capital is between £10,000 and £20,000, you must commit up to 5–10 per cent of this to every trade to make the dealing size meaningful. If you have a larger capital base of £100,000 plus, you need commit only 1–2 per cent of this to every individual trade. I have known traders put 25 per cent of their capital on every trade, and once they have taken a few big hits, they are wiped out.

When to buy

You should have a good reason for buying any stock. If, for example, the company has just jumped a regulatory hurdle, enabling it to launch a favoured new product, it bodes well. The trick is to buy early, perhaps on rumours, before the share price has fully reacted.

As a novice stock market speculator, you should favour larger companies. The shares are the most liquid, and may be traded at the narrowest spread. In recent years, many of these stocks have become volatile, which has created huge profit opportunities for traders.

Small companies are a slightly different trading proposition. They can be fantastic when you get it right because the share price can jump 30 per cent, 50 per cent or more within weeks, days or hours, entirely on sentiment. But wait until you are experienced before you trade such stocks. The shares are comparatively illiquid and, if you buy and the price plunges against you, you may find yourself as good as locked in. For more on small companies, see Day 11.

Buy shares that have relative strength, which implies a strong recent price performance compared with that of others in the sector. This should be over the past month or two, and over the past year. In such cases, the P/E ratio (see Day 7) is likely to be high.

You can calculate relative strength as follows. Divide the price of your chosen share by the figure for the Actuaries All-Share index at close of business, and the result is the relative strength ratio. Recalculate this ratio every day over some months, and plot the line on a graph. If the line is moving up, so is the share's relative strength, and vice versa. Some investment software and online services will do the work for you.

At some popular financial websites such as Interactive Investor (www.iii. co.uk), you will find details of the day's biggest winners and losers. Early in the morning, it can be profitable to invest in yesterday's *losers*, as well as in stocks that have just started rising.

As a rule of thumb, professional traders prefer the upside on any trade to be twice the downside. The worst loss that you allow should be only 2 per cent of your trading capital, which, based on trading capital of £15,000, would be £300. This way, you will have enough capital to withstand some consecutive losses.

If a stock is doing well, you may want to pyramid your position and buy more. Some traders keep buying a favoured stock in stages, but never in so large a quantity as the last time. Jesse Livermore would buy a small shareholding in a favoured stock to test the market and, if he made money on it, would take more – but only at a higher price.

When to sell

Jesse Livermore always sold shares if they started making a loss. It is a good example to follow. Most are reluctant to sell out of a losing position because it crystallizes the paper loss. They prefer to hang on in the hope that the share price will rise again.

When you buy a stock, set the percentage rise at which you plan to sell it. The share price needs to rise enough to cover your dealing costs as well as the bid–offer spread and, on share purchases, stamp duty.

You will need significant returns to make trading worthwhile. In a seven-month study, the North American Securities Association found that 70 per cent of day traders lose money.

Cut losses and run profits

In the HSL newsletter (www.hsletter.com), international trader Harry Schultz has said: 'Do professionals spend hours trying to find the next "hot" stock? No. True professionals understand that preserving original capital and not taking big losses is the secret. Don't worry about small losses.'

This brings us to a key principle of money management. Cut your losses and run your profits. This can be profitable for you even if you pick more losing than winning stocks because, under Pareto's Principle, 80 per cent of your profits will derive from 20 per cent of your trading. As speculator George Soros has said, it does not matter how often you are right when you trade, but only how much you lose when you are wrong.

To play safe, get that stop loss in place *before* you enter your trade and, if the stock declines below your cut-off point, sell automatically. As US trading guru Victor Sperandeo puts it, if an alligator has your leg, sacrifice this because, if you struggle, it will get more of your body. UK trader and seminar leader Mike Boydell has said that not using a stop loss is like running across the M25 with your head in a bucket.

The simplest stop loss is the conventional type where, if the shares should fall a given percentage below the original purchase price, you automatically sell out. I recommend that you instead use a trailing stop loss, which is reset daily against the previous day's closing price, and so trails the share price.

Your key decision is the point at which you will cut losses or stop running profits. Jesse Livermore would sell stocks when they were still rising but, on his judgement, were about to run out of momentum. For most traders, it is usual to sell a stock after the share price has started declining, and so cut the loss.

Some traders set two trailing stop losses. If the stock hits the lower stop, it serves as a warning, and you may choose to sell half your shares. At the higher stop, you must liquidate your holding.

In setting the cut-off level, consider what US trader Marty Schwartz has called in this context your *uncle* point. This is the point as in the children's game when you shout the word *uncle*, indicating that you give up.

The famous US trader William O'Neill cuts losses at 7–8 per cent below the buy price, but this is very tight and may require you to sell out on temporary dips. I suggest that you set your stop loss percentage at a maximum 15 or 20 per cent. If you are trading shares in small companies, these tend to be volatile, and a stop loss as high as 30 or 40 per cent may be needed to cover fluctuations that are not a proper trend reversal.

Occasionally the shares will have fallen too fast to get out in time, in which case you should exit at the highest price. Sell at once and ask questions afterwards.

Technical analysts have their own version of the stop loss. True to their art, it is based on share price movement as shown in the charts. One approach is to sell shares on the first technical *pullback* from a new low. This can be hard to detect.

Technical trader and guru Alan Farley has argued on Trade2win (www. trade2win.com) that you should avoid percentage stop losses because they could be wiped out by market *noise*, and they give an illusion of controlling risk, but not knowledge of the extent of the risk. Farley's case is that it is most effective to place a stop loss on top of converging resistance shown in the charts.

Do not be fooled by traders who boast that they never use a stop loss. Most will sell out quickly once the stock has started plummeting and so are applying the discipline in all but name. If you find that you are always using your stop losses, switch to buying Put options (see Day 15). I know of traders who have made this switch very profitably.

There are exceptional circumstances when you might choose not to apply your stop loss. In his book *Secrets of a Millionaire Trader*, Richard Farleigh says that you should not cut losses on an adverse price move if you understand why it happened, remain confident of a recovery and have enough capital not to sell. 'Here it may make sense to hold the position and even to consider buying more. But I would still like to see the market starting to recover before I added to a position,' he says.

This module is about trading. Do not confuse the concept with longer-term investing, which has less need for stop losses. Anthony Bolton, fund manager at Fidelity Special Situations Fund, says he does not use stop losses. 'I like to keep reassessing the story. An automatic stop loss is sometimes right and sometimes wrong. It's difficult to use on big holdings but it could make sense for individuals.'

The flip side of cutting your losses is to run your profits. This way, you can benefit from any occasion when the stock price soars beyond expectations. If it happens a few times, it will more than compensate for small losses taken in a good many other stocks. You must *dare* to let your profits mount up.

Unfortunately, some traders have a set idea of what constitutes a normal profit and feel uncomfortable if their position overreaches it. If you are in that camp, scalping may appeal. As a scalper, you aim to snatch plenty of small profits rather than to ride a few large ones. You will trade often in small sums, which means your gains will be limited in size but more frequent. You will need to do a lot of trades, and it is hard work. You may slip in and out of the same stock several times a day.

For some traders, scalping can work a treat, but for others it is like a treadmill that makes no money.

If in doubt, stay out

If you are having a run of unsuccessful trades, stop. As legendary share trader William Gann wrote in *How to Make Profits in Commodities*: 'When you make one to three trades that show losses, whether they be large or small, something is wrong with you and not the market. Your trend may have changed. My rule is to get out and wait. Study the reason for your losses.'

When markets are not doing much, it is another good time to take a break. You will have the opportunity to assess your mistakes and prepare for the next bout of trading.

Screen-based news and data

Watch short-term news and company results because they affect share prices. The more information available, and the more intense it is, the more influential it will be in the short term, according to Anthony Bolton. For seriously up-to-date news coverage, use a newswire terminal, but they are not cheap to access.

The way forward

Once you have grasped the skill of money management, and if you dedicate enough time and attention, you can succeed as a trader. But it is a different ball game from medium- to long-term investing, and fundamentals count for far less.

Dynamic rules

■ If you are trading from home, set up a dedicated office.

■ If you apply good management, you can win, even if you enter more loss-making than winning trades.

■ As a trader, do not rely too much on fundamentals.

■ Develop your own best trading system and stick to it.

■ Use limit orders and stop losses.

■ Do not have so many stocks that you cannot watch them properly.

■ Trade only with capital that you can afford to lose.

■ Expect to lose money sometimes and review losing trades.

■ Buy shares in large companies and proven high fliers. Look for relative strength, a good buying reason and an upside that is twice the downside.

■ If a stock is doing well, consider pyramiding your position and buying more.

■ If you are uncomfortable with running large profits, try scalping.

■ If you are having a run of unsuccessful trades, take a break.

■ Watch news flow and company results because they affect share prices.

How to profit from options and covered warrants

Overview

You will find enough information about options and covered warrants in this module to get you started as a trader.

We will define options and see how they can be used for speculation and hedging. I will explain the most popular trading strategies, whether as a buyer of options or, on the other side of the fence, as a writer.

We will touch upon advanced trading positions, including the butterfly and the tarantula, and how to become your own options analyst.

We will then look at covered warrants, and how they work in practice. Finally, we will touch on conventional warrants.

How options work

Options defined

An option enables you to speculate on the movement of individual shares, or of indices, currencies, commodities or interest rates. It may be used for hedging.

Options may be traded over the counter (OTC) or on exchange. The on-exchange options are cheaper because they are standardized. They are tradable without counterparty risk and are suitable for private investors.

Through an option, you have the right to buy or sell a security at a predetermined price, the exercise price, within a specified period. The market price you will have paid for the right to exercise the option is the premium, which is a small percentage of the option's size. It means the option is geared.

For every buyer of an option, there is a seller, also known as a writer. On completion of your purchase, you will pay an initial margin, which goes to the writer and will cover the worst loss that could arise in a day. You must keep this amount topped up on a day-to-day basis where necessary to sustain the level of cover. If you exercise the option, the writer must provide the underlying financial instrument at the exercise price. If you do not exercise it, the writer will have your premium.

Calls and Puts

You may have bought a *Call* option, which gives you the right, but not the obligation, to buy the underlying security at the exercise price. If the asset price is more than the exercise price of the option, the difference represents the option's value, and the option is *in the money*. If the asset price is less, the Call option is *out of the money*. If you buy an option deep *out of the money* and the underlying price moves a lot, the premium could move proportionately in percentage terms but, in absolute terms, much less.

As owner of a Call option, you will make money only if the price of the underlying stock or other financial instrument rises above the exercise price plus the premium that you paid (plus any dealing expenses). In this case, the usual way to make money is to trade your option at a profit.

You may have bought a *Put* option, which gives you the right, but not the obligation, to sell a security at the exercise price. If the exercise price is higher than the underlying security's current market price, the option is *in the money*. If it is lower, the option is *out of the money*. You will make a profit if the option price falls to below the level of the exercise price plus the premium that you have paid (plus all dealing expenses).

Intrinsic and time value

Intrinsic value is how far the underlying stock's value is above the option's exercise price, in the case of a Call option, or below it in the case of a Put option. An option has intrinsic value when it is *in the money*.

The *time value* of an option is its total value less intrinsic value. The more time an option has until it expires, the higher this figure is likely to be because the price of the underlying stock has proportionately more of a chance of changing in the option buyer's favour.

The premium consists of both intrinsic and time value, both of which can change constantly.

Shapes and sizes

Equity options come in the standard contract size of 1,000 shares, although it may vary if the underlying company is involved in a capital restructuring such as a rights issue. To find the cost of an option contract, multiply the option price by 1,000. If a Call option is priced at 70p, it will cost £700 per contract.

The options traded on Euronext.liffe, the pan-European exchange with a London presence, have expiry dates grouped three, six or nine months ahead. When a contract expires, for instance, in March, a new one is created for expiry in June. A first group of companies on Euronext.liffe has the expiry dates of January, April, July and October; a second group has February, May, August and November; and a third group expires in March, June, September and December. In any given month, options for only a third of all the companies will expire.

Index options

Options on stock market indices, known as index options, are contracts for difference (discussed generally on Day 17). They typically trade for larger amounts than equity options, perhaps several thousand pounds per contract against several hundred pounds, and they are more volatile. These factors raise the risk/reward stake.

Interest rate options

Interest rate options enable traders to speculate on, or hedge against, interest rate risk. The price level of a contract is derived by subtracting the interest rate from 100. An interest rate of 5 per cent means that the contract price is 100 — 5 = 95. Settlement is on a value per fraction of a percentage change in interest rates. The more the interest rate rises, the more the contract price declines, and the reverse.

Commodities options

Commodities react differently from stocks or bonds to market conditions and so to trade them is an excellent way to diversify your investment portfolio. Options are a good way to gain this exposure because they specify the downside risk.

Hard commodities such as oil, copper and gold move on a longer time frame than the soft commodities such as cocoa and sugar, and exposure to a basket of commodities provides its own diversification. You may achieve this by buying an option on the Dow Jones AIG Commodity Index, which trades 20 different commodities.

Basic strategies

Speculation

To speculate on options may appeal if, as an investor, you want a fast return, and are prepared to take risks to achieve it. To give yourself the best chance of success, you will need to watch the market continuously. Options are a highly liquid market, and you will usually be able to complete your trades.

Speculation through options trading is not gambling but is all about taking a calculated risk. For every buyer of an option there is a seller, but neither side has the odds intrinsically stacked in its favour.

Hedging

You can use options to hedge a position that you may have in a share or index. Hedging is different from speculation in that it is about protecting your existing position rather than making a profit. Let us look at an example of a hedging technique. If you believe the market will crash, you can buy Put options for a company in which you hold shares. This way, if the share price crashes, you can compensate by selling the Puts for a profit, and will have effectively insured your position.

Two bullish strategies

If you think the underlying security or index will rise significantly in the short term, buy a Call option. You may foresee such a rise if, for example, the underlying company has just become the target of a takeover bid or there are rumours to that effect.

A riskier alternative strategy is to become the writer of a Put option. This way, you will receive the premium from the buyer. Usually, the Put option sold will expire worthless, and you will keep the premium (10–15 per cent of the gain) without having to buy the underlying stock.

However, if the share price falls below the exercise price (plus the option buyer's dealing expenses), you stand to lose money. The price of the underlying share cannot fall below zero pence and so your maximum loss will be the full value of the share. City professionals do not like writing Put options. I know of a City trader who lost a fortune this way at the start of the market correction of high-tech stocks in March and April 2000, although, in all fairness, some have fared a lot better.

Two bearish strategies

If you think that the company's share price will fall hard, your simplest strategy is to buy a Put option. As an alternative, you could *write* a Call option. If so, you will take the premium from the buyer, which is the main attraction of the deal, and you will keep it if, as usually happens, the share price does not rise above the exercise price (plus the option buyer's dealing expenses). If the share price does rise above this level, you are faced with a theoretical unlimited loss because you will have to provide the shares at however high a valuation they have reached.

If you are writing a covered Call, you will own the shares already and will simply provide them without any further cash outlay. What is riskier is when you have written a Naked Call, which means you do not own the underlying shares. If the share price collapses, you will then have to buy shares at the prevailing market price to keep your part of the deal. The same principle applies in reverse to writing Puts (see above).

Straddle

A common option trading strategy is a straddle. Use it when you expect the underlying stock to move significantly, but you don't know in which direction.

In a *long* straddle, you will buy a Call option and Put option at identical exercise prices and expiration dates. It sounds a wonderful compromise. The catch is that the share price has to move up or down a lot – to get past the expense of two premiums rather than the usual one (as well as the high commission costs applicable to a straddle) – if you are to make money.

Advanced strategies

Wheeling and dealing

Professional options traders use other, in some cases far more complex, techniques. For instance, under a *break forwards*, the options buyer can break the contract with the writer. Under *participating forwards*, the buyer can benefit from the *upside* of an option while having some protection from the *downside*.

Butterflies and condors

If you imagined that bulls and bears were the only animals in the stock market farmyard, think again. Market professionals use various combinations of Puts and Calls to protect their positions while they speculate on the future direction of a stock or index. One such strategy is the *butterfly*, which uses four options and three exercise prices. Alternatively, there is the *condor* spread, also known as the *top hat* spread.

Spider power

The *tarantula* is an options strategy that can be as formidable as it sounds. This spider has eight legs, each representing different futures and options contracts that expire on the same date. If a contract lapses, a leg *breaks* but it can *heal*. If several legs are damaged, the tarantula can become *crippled*, but may recover when markets turn volatile.

Alternatively, a second tarantula may be introduced with thicker legs that correct the failed legs of its predecessor. In this case, the spiders are said to have *mated*.

For a list of further such techniques, with succinct explanations, visit the options strategies page of Sucden at www.sucden.co.uk.

Risk warnings

Derivatives abuse

Options can be bad for your wealth if they lead to gambling, where, by definition, the odds are stacked against you, as distinct from the calculated risks of speculation.

The scandals are few but big. There is no doubt that determined individuals can always find a way to abuse derivatives. It is by now well documented how trader Nick Leeson took huge risks on derivatives and brought down Barings, the investment bank where he worked.

Leeson was the star trader and general manager in the bank's Singapore office and, as it turned out, he was inadequately supervised. The 28-year-old's trading strategy was based on arbitrage, which was to profit from price differentials between the same strategies on different markets.

In January 1995, Leeson started writing Put and Call options on the Nikkei 225 index at the same exercise price. It created a straddle and Barings would keep the premiums only if the index stayed within the 19,000–21,000 trading range. Chance dictated otherwise and, when on 17 January Kobe and Osaka were hit by a huge earthquake, the Nikkei 225 fell too far. On 23 January, it had dipped to 17,950.

Leeson started buying March and June 95 futures contracts, which were a bet on an improvement in the market. It was another gamble that went wrong. The Nikkei 225 deteriorated further, and eventually Barings had lost more than £800 million, which was more than its capital, and in 1995, it collapsed.

The event triggered consideration of the Bank of England's role of supervising banks, which was later transferred to the Financial Services Authority. The Bank has retained responsibility for the stability of the banking system.

It is such events that have led to a public perception, fuelled by the media, that derivatives are dangerous. Warren Buffett, considered the world's greatest stock market investor, has called derivatives 'weapons of mass destruction'. City professionals unsurprisingly take a more lenient view and note that hedging through derivatives reduces rather than creates risk.

Become your own options analyst

Strategy

As a trader in equity options, you should be valuing the underlying stocks. Use fundamental analysis (Day 7) and technical analysis (Days 8, 9 and 10).

Also watch Put–Call ratios. When there are many more buyers of Calls than Puts on equities, the Put–Call ratio is low, but you can expect, more often than not, a reversal leading to a market decline. Conversely, when investors are buying Puts and the Put–Call ratio is high, you may expect Call buyers to emerge and the market to rise again.

When you buy, select those options on shares and indices that are volatile enough to provide a good chance of the big move in your favour. It means paying more for the option.

Generally, options are more expensive when interest rates are in decline because investors are then willing to withdraw cash from deposit accounts for trading purposes. To reduce your risk in trading, you can buy options on a variety of securities and they can be both Calls and Puts.

Black–Scholes

Buyers and sellers ultimately set the price of an option, but it is City traders who value it. One of the standard ways is through the Black–Scholes model, which is based on the work of two US academics, Fisher Black and Myron Scholes. The model was first published in 1973 and it uses a complex mathematical formula, taking into account the intrinsic value and time value of the option and the fact that it does not pay dividends. A limitation of Black–Scholes is that it assumes that the stock price moves randomly because it reflects the full knowledge and expectations of investors. This is in accordance with the efficient market hypothesis, which is widely disputed.

Black–Scholes was a basis for some aggressive derivatives strategies of Long Term Capital Management (LTCM), a hedge fund founded by ex-Salomon Brothers trader John Meriwether, and Myron Scholes was one of its main shareholders. When asked whether he believed in efficient markets, Meriwether furiously replied: 'I *make* them efficient.'

It worked in the early days. In 1995, LTCM gave shareholders a 42.8 per cent return and, in 1996, a 40.8 per cent return. In 1997, it had more than halved to 17.1 per cent, which was still very healthy but, in 1998, the fund failed and the US Federal Reserve bailed it out.

It is unfair to blame Black–Scholes for the collapse because LTCM had operated on a large enough scale to make it untypical, according to the pundits. The City still believes in Black–Scholes but sometimes modifies it. Traders exploit anomalies in options priced according to the model.

Online learning and research

So far, we have looked briefly at how options work, and have covered the important points. If you decide to explore options further, the internet is your friend. Surf selectively because many sites on options try to sell you software or courses.

Visit The Futures and Options Association, the industry's trade body, at www.foa.co.uk, and download high-quality, free material.

It is worth visiting the Chicago Board Options Exchange at www.cboe.com. The site has useful free educational material.

Covered warrants

A market for private investors

Covered warrants differ from options in that they are not contracts, but the two types of derivative have plenty in common. The covered warrant is an exchange-traded packaged derivative mainly for private investors and is *covered* because the issuer simultaneously buys the underlying stock or financial instrument.

The product has flourished for some years in continental Europe. It was only in late 2002 that the London Stock Exchange (LSE) introduced it to the UK with a perceived aim of obtaining a significant presence in derivatives. In London so far, covered warrants, except in the FTSE-100 index, have made slow progress.

To trade in this product, you will pay a small premium, which gives you the right to buy or sell the underlying asset. As with options, covered warrants are split into Calls and Puts and, as time passes, they become less valuable, which is reflected in a declining premium. Every covered warrant is normally traded before its maturity date.

The biggest turnoff about covered warrants is that they are expensive compared with, for example, options. The compensating factor is that they are user-friendly. Covered warrants cannot be shorted, which is another limitation. But unlike in spread bets or CFDs, you cannot lose more than 100 per cent of your money. It is a significant advantage to the type of unsophisticated investor that is typically attracted to the product. At the end of their term, covered warrants that are *in* the money are automatically closed.

No stamp duty is payable on your purchase of a covered warrant, and as owner, you will receive no dividend from the underlying share. You will be liable to capital gains tax on any profits.

Some warrants are traded on the Central Warrants Trading Service platform, which is part of SETS, the LSE's electronic order book, and the product may generally be traded via retail service providers (see Days 3 and 4).

Conventional warrants

The conventional warrant is a different animal from the covered warrant. It may be used to buy a specified number of *new* shares in a company at a specified exercise price either at a given time, or within a given period.

Companies like to issue conventional warrants because they do not have to include them on the balance sheet. Warrants tend to rise and fall in value with the underlying shares, sometimes exaggerating the movement. They are not part of a company's share capital and so have no voting rights.

Sometimes the warrants are packaged as a sweetener to accompany a bond issue. Capital gains tax is payable on profits.

The way forward

We have seen how you may use derivatives for hedging. For speculators they are a high-risk game. Be cautious.

Dynamic rules

- ■ You may use options for speculating or hedging.
- ■ Exchange-traded options are suitable for private investors because, unlike over-the-counter options, they are standardized, and have no counterparty risk.
- ■ You can buy Call options, which give you the right to buy, or Put options, which give you the right to sell.
- ■ For every options buyer, there is a seller, also known as a writer, and neither side has the odds in its favour.
- ■ Equity options have a standard contact size of 1,000 shares. To find the cost of an option contract, multiply the option price by 1,000.
- ■ Use commodities to diversify your equity portfolio. Options are a good way to do it because the downside risk is specified.
- ■ Index options trade for larger amounts than equity options and are more volatile.
- ■ Commodity options are a good way to diversify your equities portfolio because they specify the downside risk.
- ■ A straddle is an options strategy where you take two opposing positions simultaneously. You will expect the underlying stock to move significantly but you don't know in which direction.
- ■ Options can be bad for your wealth if they lead you to gambling.
- ■ In valuing equity options, assess the underlying stocks.
- ■ Watch the Put–Call ratio and, when it is significantly high or low, trade in anticipation of a reversal.
- ■ The City uses the Black–Scholes model to value options. The model takes into account intrinsic and time value and the non-

payment of dividends. A limitation is that it assumes stock prices move randomly.

■ Covered warrants are an exchange-traded derivative rather like options. The product is expensive and cannot be shorted but it is user-friendly. Traders cannot lose more money than they put up.

■ The conventional warrant may be used to buy new shares in a company at a specified price and time.

The daredevil trader: financial futures and spread betting

Overview

In this module we will look briefly at financial futures. We will then focus on spread betting, which can be based on futures or, as an alternative, on cash markets.

Financial futures

Futures are a binding agreement to buy or sell a given quantity of an asset by a specified future date. Dealing is through a contract, which is between two parties to buy and sell the underlying instrument in a specific quantity at a pre-arranged date at an agreed price.

A futures contract could be in commodities such as cocoa, coffee or corn, and will be a paper investment. You can, but never have to, take delivery of the underlying product. Since the 1970s, there have been financial futures, some of which are available in small-size contracts designed for the private investor. They are based on a financial instrument such as a bond, share, index, interest rate or currency. The agreement is to exchange a cash sum reflecting the difference between the initial price of the underlying asset and its price on settlement.

If you trade financial futures, you may speculate on the price of your chosen instrument rising or falling. Otherwise you may hedge against potential losses on your main portfolio with an opposite position in futures. The market is highly liquid and you will pay only small commissions in relation to the deal size.

Like other derivatives, futures are highly geared, so you may trade a much larger sum than the amount you have put up. You will put up around 10 per cent of the contract as initial margin. Your broker may draw on your margin account if you should incur losses but will add any profits to it. Should your account become depleted, you must top it up with *variation* margin. In practice, many successful traders close out their position and take a loss before that point is reached. They also commonly use stop losses (see Day 14).

A user-friendly way to trade on the value of financial futures is through financial spread betting.

Spread betting

The basics

Financial spread betting is a way to trade on the movement of stocks, indices or other financial instruments. You may make bets on futures of the products, or sometimes on the underlying cash products. Spread bets are accessible even to the least sophisticated traders, and they may commit only small sums of money.

In technical terms, financial spread betting is an over-the-counter market, and the party issuing the bet is always the counterparty. The firms are regulated by the Financial Services Authority (FSA), which has shown its teeth in cracking down on misleading advertising from the industry under its 'Treating customers fairly' requirements.

The financial bookmakers are execution-only, which means they cannot advise you on how, or whether, to bet, although they may offer you data and working examples to help you. Like online stockbrokers, they do little more than take your order.

Traders who use spread betting firms are almost entirely male, with a leaning towards the 25–35-year-old age group, particularly those who work in information technology (IT), surveys have found,

You may place a bet with a firm based on your belief that a share price, an index, interest rates or similar will move in a certain direction. Spread bets are geared, which means that although you trade on movements in either the underlying financial instrument or its futures, you need only put up initial

Spread Betting with Cantor Index

With Cantor Index you are spread betting with a name you can rely on. Cantor Index Limited is part of the global Cantor Fitzgerald Group of Companies, a premier global financial services provider with 50 years as a recognised leader and expert in the specialised areas of equity and fixed income capital markets.

Our presence all over the world enables us to offer bets on a wide range of products from shares and indices to bonds and commodities in every market.

At Cantor Index our objective is to provide all our clients with a high level of professional support, whether you are an experienced spread bettor or a beginner. We take pride in offering advanced levels of professionalism and we are viewed as a market leader in terms of offering clients the latest technology. Our online trading platform "Pulse" is regularly upgraded and improved providing our clients with access to a superior spread betting service. Cantor Mobile is the most advanced mobile spread betting platform. This offers all the convenience of online trading through a number of sophisticated handheld computers. You can check prices, follow the latest financial news, spread bet in real-time and manage your account wherever you are.

Why spread bet with Cantor Index?

There are many advantages spread betting has over conventional share dealing. You pay no fees, commission or stamp duty and all your gains are tax free.* Also you can profit from falling as well as rising markets as we always give a two-way price so you can 'sell' short or 'buy' long.

You can spread bet real-time online and benefit from our portfolio management system, live prices and up-to the minute financial news.

When you make a financial spread bet, you never actually own the stock, bond, commodity or share. Instead you 'buy' our quote when you bet that the market will rise, or 'sell' our quote when betting that the price will fall. Spread betting is effectively leverages trading, you can control a significant position in the market with a relatively small deposit. Unlike fixed odds betting, if the market subsequently goes up (or down) as you predicted, your winnings multiply. If the market moves in the opposite direction to your prediction, then your losses will multiply.

For example, if you think Vodafone's share value will rise, then you might buy £10 per penny which is the equivalent of buying 1000 shares.

Our quote is 172-174 and you buy at £5 at 174. Vodafone's share price does indeed rise and a few weeks later you decide to take our tax free profit; our revised quote is 194-196 so you close out by selling at 194. Your have therefore make 20 points (194-174=20) which at £5 per penny generates a £100 profit (20 x £5=£100).

If the market had moved against you our Vodafone quote fell to 154-156 and you felt that the price would drop further then you might accept your losses at that level and close at 154 realising £100 loss. If you think that the share price will recover but the expiry date of the trade is approaching you can decide to extend the contract through to the next month of the March, June, September and December cycle.

Spread Betting made easier with Cantor Index Accounts

Cantor Index offers two types of account, deposit accounts and credit accounts. With a deposit account, you must deposit funds into account to cover your total NTR, plus any movements against you in the market you are betting on.

A credit account can offer you a waived NTR facility, which means that you can open bets with a total NTR up to this limit, without the need to deposit funds. To open an account online please go to cantorindex.co.uk.

Spread betting with Cantor Index is available Sunday 11.00pm to Friday 9.15pm and dealing is instant, so the price we quote is the price you get. We do offer guaranteed stop-loss facilities on certain stocks and options to allow you to limit potential losses. For more information please call **020 7894 7894** or email **cs@cantorindex.co.uk**

Spread bets are high risk products; you need deposit only a small percentage of the value of the bet. However, your losses may substantially exceed that deposit very rapidly and thus require you to make additional deposits at short notice to maintain your bets. Spread bets are not suitable for all customers. Before betting, you should ensure you fully understand the risks and seek independent financial advice if necessary.

Cantor Index Limited is authorised and regulated by the Financial Services Authority

*Tax laws may change and can differ depending upon your individual circumstances, in particular if you pay tax in a jurisdiction outside the UK.

margin, perhaps 10–15 per cent of the underlying value. You may need to top up this margin regularly so that your position remains covered, should it have moved against you. You will make or gain as a percentage of the underlying financial instrument rather than of your margin. The price movement may wipe out your margin or more, or increase it considerably.

Forward or cash bets

In the past, almost all bets were on futures and options which, by anticipating movements, are likely to move faster than the underlying share price. This has worked for the traditional bookie approach, which is to calculate risk and add it to profit. CMC Markets came into the business as an established foreign exchange market maker, assessing the risk as the price is calculated and offering this price to the market. In 2002, it started 'Daily rolling cash bets', where the basis for pricing a spread bet is the cash price of the underlying instrument rather than the futures contract. Another feature of this bet is that there is no fixed expiry and each contract is automatically rolled into the next day. This type of bet covers 96 per cent of CMC Markets' business, and other large bookmakers now offer a similar product, at least on large stocks and indices. 'There is a convergence between us and the traditional bookie types now,' says Jayne Banks, marketing manager at CMC Markets.

Rolling cash bets have a much tighter spread – the difference between the buying and selling price – than forward bets, ie bets on futures. The spread on cash bets can be the same as when you buy directly in the cash market. For example, a rolling cash bet on Vodafone has a spread of a quarter of a point at the time of writing, which is the same as if you bought the shares directly.

Spreads, even when as narrow as this, are a way in which spread betting firms make their money. A second way is through overnight lending charges to traders on rolling cash bets, which are based on 100 per cent of the underlying money, regardless of how much the trader has put up on margin. This charge is typically LIBOR (London Interbank Offered Rate) – an interest rate at which banks can borrow funds, in marketable size, from other banks – plus a percentage, perhaps 2 or 3 per cent, which is then divided by 365 representing days of the year, so amounting to a typically small sum per day. But on an aggregate basis from all customers, this is profitable for the spread betting firm. As a flipside, if the trader takes a short position (defined and discussed later in this chapter), it is the *firm* that pays interest on overnight positions. A third way in which a spread betting firm makes money is that it does not pay interest on deposit accounts where margin is placed, or it pays a low rate on sizeable amounts deposited, which means it can use the money to generate extra returns for itself.

Traders taking a spread bet in futures do not have to pay overnight borrowing charges, but the spreads are larger. In this case, the spreads must cover a built-in *cost of carry* as well as expenses and the firm's profit margin. As large spread betting firm IG Index says in its literature, 'forward prices trade at a premium to spot prices to reflect the sacrifice of interest which an investor experiences by making payment for actual shares instead of taking a forward position'. But if shares are expected to go dividend before the forward dealing date, the forward price will be reduced accordingly, it notes.

These large spreads can make forward spread betting less cost-effective than contracts for difference (CFDs) (see Day 17). Critics say the spreads are opaque and are sometimes over-inflated, which doubtless is why spread betting has traditionally been a market for amateurs, focused on user-friendliness.

Indeed, from the horse's mouth, the industry's own advice is that, when you ask for the usual two-way quote on the telephone, you should not, in your own interest, reveal whether you are a buyer or a seller.

But it is possible for traders to work the system effectively. 'If you are going to trade short term, cash bets can be cost-effective, but after that, borrowing costs may mount up too much and you may be better off with futures bets, although individual situations can be different,' the early morning person at the IG Index help desk tells me.

In all trades, you will pay neither fees nor commission to the spread betting firm, although spreads are absolutely at the bookmakers' discretion. When you give your order, you may nominate a unit stake which, on a small transaction, is typically £2–£5 a single point.

You can bet on a wide range of financial instruments, but shares and indices are the most popular. 'People trade shares more than indices but tend to hold them longer. Trading in indices is more active over a short period,' says Banks of CMC Markets.

Taking a short position

To sell short is to sell an investment that you do not own that you will buy back later – at a profit, you hope – to meet the requirement to deliver the shares. The opportunity is effectively closed to private investors in conventional share trading, due to the short standard settlement period. But spread betting and CFDs make it possible to take a short position.

If you are convinced an index or share will go down sharply, you can take a short position and, if you are right, make money. This gives you far more flexibility than if you can only take a long position.

Multiple exposures

Spread bets are available in foreign exchange, treasuries, commodities and other products, allowing multiple exposures. You can trade US stocks, and UK stocks after hours, through American Depositary Receipts (certificates issued by a US bank representing shares in a foreign stock that is traded on a US exchange). The spread betting firm may hedge its own position, which is when it offsets one trade with another. For this purpose, the firm uses futures, and sometimes also CFDs.

Let me deviate for a moment to explain how markets are interrelated, something which is relevant for all types of trading in stock and other financial markets, and not just spread betting.

Mining stocks in the FTSE-100 are a play on base metal, precious metal and oil prices (including related futures), and the oil stocks, including BP and Royal Dutch Shell and, in a different way, Cairn Energy, are heavily affected by the oil price. Together, miners and oils make up well over 30 per cent of the FTSE-100 index by market capitalization. This is not a bad place to start trading. If oil and metal prices rise, so miners tend to, and if the prices decline, the stocks are likely to go with them.

This is, of course, a major generalization as there are many other factors that influence the price, including, for instance, whether it has run up too high in previous days, leaving investors ready to take profits. If, for example, you trade mining stocks, you must take individual characteristics into account. Kazakhmys is a Kazakhstan-based mining company. It is a play on the copper price and has country-specific issues, including corporate governance risks. Anglo American is more diversified and is subject to takeover speculation, which can create share price volatility, but it has put in place a defensive strategy, including cash returns to shareholders and restructuring. Lonmin has interests in platinum and Xstrata in nickel.

The relevant metal prices may change throughout the day based partly on trading on the London Metal Exchange. What this means is that the miners can start the day well up and end it well down, and although they tend to run together, there are exceptions. To trade these stocks effectively, you need to understand where the business specializes and to watch the metal and oil prices.

Oil supply restrictions drive up the oil price, both US crude and in London, increasing inflationary pressure. Another inflationary signal, one of many, is good manufacturing output figures. If such figures come from the United States, they will have a knock-on effect in Europe, bearing in mind that over 70 per cent of the FTSE-100 earnings are from outside the UK, of which the

United States is part. Weak sterling can help exports by making British goods cheaper abroad, so currency plays a part in the overall picture.

The danger of inflationary pressures is that they can force central banks, including the US Federal Reserve and the Bank of England, to raise interest rates, which makes it more expensive for quoted companies to borrow money and, as we have seen on Day 7, acts as a dampener on the stock market. The prospects of higher interest rates can send bond yields up to match what is anticipated, and the corollary of this is that bond prices would come down proportionately, as yield is a percentage of price.

It is easy, then, to see how financial markets are interrelated. What counts most for markets is the *prospect* of a price or rate move rather than the move itself. The market discounts likely events in advance, although surprises can rock the boat. When the London stock market starts trading at 8.30 am, Wall Street will not open until the afternoon, but we can make an educated guess as to whether the US Dow Jones index will open up or down, and roughly how far, by looking at, among other things, futures, any economic figures, how Wall Street closed the previous day and how Asian markets performed overnight.

As at September 2006, shortly before this book went to press, US growth and corporate earnings are showing signs of slowing, in manufacturing and other areas as well as housing, which could lead to a delay in a much-feared interest rate rise.

If the US Federal Reserve resists an interest rate hike, so may the UK in turn. An understanding of such knock-on effects, and of currency issues such as how the US dollar has been supported by emerging markets, is incredibly useful for getting a full picture. You can get much of the latest thinking in clear, non-technical language from reading the weekly magazine *The Economist* (www.economist.com).

In general, given that in spread betting you can take a short as well as a long position, you will make money out of volatility. There are stocks that are particularly volatile, like PartyGaming, the online gaming group, which has fluctuated dramatically on news related to changes in US legislation. For the brave it has offered trading opportunities.

Spread Betting. What is it, how does it work and how can you profit from it?

 David Jones is Chief Market Analyst at CMC Markets and is a regular commentator on television channels such as CNBC and the BBC.

Spread Betting has been around for more than 30 years, but it is probably in the last five years that it has really grabbed the attention of the private investor and become a viable way of trading instruments such as shares, stock indices, currencies and commodities.

Spread Betting may not suitable for everyone because it carries a high risk to your capital due to the fact that it is a margined product – but it is not just exclusive to high-flying city professionals. With Spread Betting there is no commission to pay; no stamp duty and any profits are tax free (tax laws can of course change). The minimum bet size has dropped in recent years – with CMC Markets for example you can trade from as low as £1 per point.

Spread Betting lets you take positions on shares and the major stock market indices around the world. Alternative financial markets to equities also prove popular, with Spread Betting opening up currencies and commodities such as gold and oil which are very popular with our clients.

First of all we will start with the basic concepts. For individuals who have bought and sold shares in the past it is not a quantum leap to understand how Spread Betting works. The Spread Betting companies will quote a price based on an underlying financial instrument, which updates in real time as the market changes in price. Spread Betting companies quote a "two way" price – in the same way as with individual shares there is a price you can sell at (the bid price) and a price you can buy at (the offer price). As a client, if you think the price of the market is going to go up you buy; if you think it is going to fall you can sell. The latter is known as short-selling and gives you the opportunity to profit if you think a financial market or individual share is going to fall in price.

With most Spread Betting companies there are various orders you can place (usually free of charge) such as stops and limits that will help minimise risk and automatically exit positions for you if a certain level gets reached.

The main difference between Spread Betting and, for example, buying or selling shares or futures is that you do not deal in so many shares or contracts, but in "pounds per point". It is important to understand what a point constitutes in the various markets available. With UK shares for example it is usually a one penny move. So, if the Vodafone Spread Bet quote goes up 5p in one day then that is a five point move. If our investor has bought £5 per point, that move translates into a £25 point profit. If he has sold £5 per point thinking Vodafone will drop, then that five point rise translates into a £25 loss for the day. If you are not sure what a one point move is in the market you are interested in then call your spread betting company – they will only be too happy to help.

CMC Markets is a world-leading provider of Spread Betting, CFDs and FX and is committed to providing its clients with tight spreads and competitive margin rates. To find out more about trading with CMC Markets, please contact Freefone **08000 933 633** or visit **www.cmcmarkets.co.uk**. CMC Markets regularly runs free seminars on how to trade CFDs and Spread Betting so visit our website for further details.

Remember Spread Betting, CFDs and FX are leveraged products and carry a high level of risk to your capital. It is possible to incur losses that exceed your initial investment. These products may not be suitable for all investors, therefore ensure you fully understand the risks involved and seek independent advice if necessary.

CMC Markets UK Plc and CMC Spreadbet Plc are authorised and regulated by the Financial Services Authority.

Closing your position

The difference between the price at which you placed your bet and at which you close it out will be your profit or loss. If you have made a gain, the firm will deposit it into your account. You can take as large a position as you like, provided you put up the required margin, but the spread betting firm may require you to trade a minimum £1 per point.

Costs

Spread betting has two major advantages over investing directly in the stock market. You will pay no stamp duty on purchases and profits will be free of any applicable capital gains tax (CGT). The tax advantage is the only significant reason why some switch from spot trading foreign exchange (see Day 17) to spread bets given the spreads are the same, financial book makers say. It can work in reverse. Some may go for CFDs, because it means they can offset capital gains tax losses against CGT.

A market mostly for speculators

You may use spread betting, like other derivatives, for hedging but it mostly attracts speculators. Some canny speculators have two or three accounts with financial bookmakers in an effort to get the keenest prices. You cannot enter a bet with one firm and close it with another, but you can enter two bets simultaneously with different firms.

Select the right financial bookmaker

Spread betting firms understandably try to entice you into opening an account with them. With the FSA regulating the industry, it is not in firms' interest to get anybody trading without understanding the risks and how to control them, and there is a move towards educating the public in these techniques. The larger spread betting firms run free educational seminars.

Take advantage of these to get to grips with the basics of spread betting. You will find that the styles of training delivery can vary. Two of the best seminar leaders are Tom Hougaard, chief market strategist at City Index, and David Jones, chief market analyst at CMC Markets. Tom delivers informative seminars in something of a salesman's style. David has a perhaps more cerebral, more traditionally educative approach.

If you decide that spread betting is for you, find a financial bookmaker suitable for your type of trading (you will find a list in the appendix). If you want a punt on the FTSE-100 index, you will have a wide choice of firms.

If you want to place a more unusual bet, you may do best to go to IG Index (www.igindex.co.uk), which is the longest-established financial bookmaker and offers a particularly wide range of bets. If you want to place a low-size bet, Finspreads (www.finspreads.com) is a good firm to use and, if you want rolling cash bets, CMC Markets (www.cmcmarkets.com) is strong.

Control your risk

If you plan to speculate through spread betting, set aside dedicated capital that you can afford to lose. Make some small bets initially and get used to the market.

As in other derivatives, it makes sense to use a stop loss, which the firm should apply on your behalf free of charge. Be warned that a financial instrument can fall too fast for you to apply the stop at the set percentage level. The reliable solution is to use a *guaranteed* stop (unavailable on traded options), but you will pay a premium for this in the form of a wider spread.

Consider using a limit order to close a profitable bet at a predetermined level. Some traders place a limit order and stop loss on the same trade, so defining the maximum profit or loss.

Two specialist trading strategies

Let me explain two common specialist trading strategies. The first strategy is pairs trading, otherwise known as spread trading or dual trading, and it is also widely used in CFDs. This is when you invest in the performance of one stock against a correlated stock. It is a form of arbitrage enabling you to profit from the divergence.

An example of this strategy is when you go long on a stock that seems likely to outperform, and simultaneously go short on a stock that seems likely to fall in value. You are hedged and so maintain a position of market neutrality. If the market goes in one direction, you will gain on the long investment but lose on the short.

The two stocks should be highly correlated, which means from the same sector. As a result, they will react to the same industry events. The stocks should be trading outside their historical range and, ideally, will be making an unusual divergence. You could go long on BP and short on Royal Dutch Shell with the possibility of making a profit irrespective of how the FTSE-100 performs.

You must treat the two transactions as one trade, investing the same money in each stock, and opening and closing both trades simultaneously. If, as you expect, the long stock outperforms the short stock, irrespective of the absolute direction, you will have gained. If both stocks move significantly up or down,

you will ultimately gain because one side can appreciate ad infinitum and the other can fall in value only as far as zero. But your profit comes only after you have paid two sets of commissions.

The second strategy is to take a long position on stocks that are expected to enter the FTSE-100 index following the quarterly review of its constituents. Companies with a market capitalization at 111th place or below by size are relegated from the FTSE-100, and companies that have risen to the 90th place or above are promoted to it.

If you are to follow this strategy, you should go long in the anticipated entrant to the FTSE-100 a few days before the entrants are formally named. You should sell your position the night before the stock enters the FTSE, which is often the catalyst for a sharp decline in the share price. As a parallel strategy, you could short stocks likely to be relegated from the FTSE-100 and then reverse your position. To keep abreast of changes in the index, see the FTSE International website (www.ftse.com).

Your chances

Here comes the shocking bit. I have seen punters lose tens of thousands of pounds in this game, sometimes on one deal, and this is the tip of the iceberg. Informal industry feedback suggests that at least 90 per cent of unsophisticated traders lose money on some popular index trades, which is similar to figures often cited for other derivatives. I have discussed this figure with spread betting firms and some are reluctant to concede it is as great as this. But they cannot specify overall gains or losses because they don't know how much hedging is going on.

Independent training

My advice to you is to avoid independent training on spread betting unless you are sure of the credentials of the trainer. I know of a financial fraudster who served a sentence in a young offenders' institution for financial fraud and, on release, he set up a financial training and newsletter business that was eventually to concentrate on spread betting.

To help sell his expensive advisory services, this bright spark produces paperwork that provides *evidence* of his personal gains in spread betting. He has obtained it by the tactic of placing enormous bets through two spread betting firms at once, on opposite ways. If the market shifts significantly, as in some cases it does, one bet will gain heavily, and the other lose by as much. He will sell out of both bets, breaking even except for the costs incurred from the spreads.

The trainer photocopies only the paperwork that represents the *winning* bet and mails it to his potential customers as claimed irrefutable evidence of his successful recent track record in financial spread betting. He repeats the trick regularly. The apparent track record makes a lot of difference when this master of duplicity is persuading someone to part with nearly £2,500 for a one-day seminar on spread betting, particularly given that he has no formal qualifications and has never worked for a blue-chip firm as a trader. Even after significant marketing expenses, the returns on his seminars are huge. He supplements them with a subscription newsletter, full of sincere-sounding spiel, simplistic charting ideas, and opinion, always laced with statements about how much money he makes from his own trading.

As in any area of the investment business, some make far more money from giving advice than from putting it into practice. Unfortunately, some of the reputable spread betting and financial information or software firms have teamed up with the cowboy seminar leaders because they wanted the business flow. They have since largely backed off for the sake of reputation but underlying links often remain. For more warnings about financial services training, see Day 18.

The way forward

Let us now sum up. Spread betting is user-friendly and you can trade in small sizes, which can make it a good entry point for traders. But it is opaque and it can be expensive if you take all costs into account, although with rolling cash bets, the spreads are narrow. Charles Vintcent is a stockbroker with a specialist interest in spread betting and at seminars he has advised taking bets only to make fun money. For more about this expert's approach, visit Topspreadbets (www.topspreadbets.com).

Let us look into the old crystal ball, a familiar activity for the financial services industry. Spread betting is likely to expand much faster as larger institutions get involved. It has already been taking some of the *active* trading away from online stockbrokers. There are 400,000 financial spread betting accounts open today, but, with an annual 25 per cent growth rate, the numbers could rise to 1 million people by 2011 if spread betting broadens its appeal, according to a June 2006 white paper commissioned by Finspreads and authored by two academics of Cass Business School.

How far spread betting can go depends partly on whether its marketing and educational initiatives overcome the stigma attached to betting, say industry sources. It is unlikely that it will reach beyond the UK in the foreseeable future because of difficulties in online gaming legislation in other countries. In contrast, CFDs (see Day 17) have an international presence.

Dynamic rules

- Financial futures are a highly liquid market open to private investors.

- Financial spread betting is an over-the-counter market where you may bet mainly on futures or options in the underlying instrument.

- The financial bookmakers make their profit on the spread, on holding money without paying interest and on lending money.

- Rolling cash spread bets have narrower spreads than forward spread bets, but you must pay overnight lending costs.

- There is no stamp duty on spread betting and, unlike on contracts for difference, profits are free of any applicable capital gains tax.

- You will protect yourself against losses best by using a stop loss or, more reliably but at a cost, a guaranteed stop loss.

- Before you spread bet, understand risk management techniques, including use of stop losses.

- A common strategy for spread betting and derivatives is pairs trading, which is to invest in the performance of one stock against another.

- Another strategy is to trade CFDs in stocks entering or leaving the FTSE-100 index.

- Avoid commercial training in spread betting unless you are sure of the trainer's credentials.

The canny margin trader: contracts for difference and foreign exchange

Overview

In this module we will look first at the contract for difference, which is now very similar to spread bets but can under some circumstances be cheaper, and is a product accessible only to more sophisticated investors. You should read this chapter in conjunction with Day 16.

Next, we will focus on foreign exchange, which technology has made accessible to private investors at competitive costs.

Contracts for difference

The product

The contract for difference (CFD) is a contract between two parties to exchange the difference between the opening and closing price of a contract, as at the contract's close, multiplied by the specified number of shares. It is a neat way to get exposure to the price movement in, among other things, a stock or index without ever owning the underlying instrument. If the share price goes up or down, you will make or lose money on the difference.

Like spread betting, this is an over-the-counter market, which means the counterparty is the product issuer. A guaranteed stop loss is similarly available at a premium. But unlike spread bets, the CFD aims to replicate all the financial benefits of share ownership except for voting rights. You will be entitled to dividend payments and, depending on your broker, will have full access to corporate actions, including rights issues and takeover activity. There are CFDs based on indices, currencies and commodities.

The CFD market now accounts for more than 20 per cent of trading by volume on the London Stock Exchange, and the product is now commonly offered by spread betting firms, CFD market makers, specialist brokers and online dealers. Since the first edition of this book was published in 2002, CFDs have expanded their coverage to include almost any market or any kind of asset. You can typically trade CFDs in all UK stocks with a market capitalization (share price × number of shares in issue) of over £50 million, in many US and European stocks, and in all major world indices.

The market

The market attracts institutional investors, particularly the hedge funds – those freewheeling spirits that trade using sophisticated techniques in pursuit of absolute returns. The CFD enables them to take a position in equities without revealing their identities. By direct market access (DMA) through brokers you can, as a trader, obtain often keener prices than through spread betting firms acting as market makers, provided somebody on the other side is prepared to meet the trade, but your deals will have to be of a specified minimum size.

Not everybody has an appetite for DMA, where a commission must be paid and there is not the added liquidity which a market maker can bring. But unless you use DMA, you are often just as well off doing spread betting (see Day 16).

In recent years, private investors have become increasingly involved in CFDs, but, unlike on spread bets, CFDs are open only to intermediate customers under current FSA classifications, which means that to trade this product, you must have some experience and knowledge.

Trading

As with other derivatives, you will trade the CFD on margin. At the start of the trade, you will put up initial margin, which is often at least 10 per cent of the value of the underlying instrument. The smaller the stock size, the greater the

‹GL◉BAL TRADER›
WELCOME TO THE NEW WORLD
www.gt247.com

Global Trader

Global Trader was established in 2000. It brought trading to your doorstep by providing tailored leveraged brokerage execution services, through CFDs, to the world's financial markets.

Global Trader provides personalised service and Direct Market Access coupled with extensive middle and back office integration. This is supported by world-class risk management and local market coverage. It's your ticket to the new world, and you're travelling first class.

Great benefits
- Independence
- Anonymity
- Direct Market Access
- Straight through processing

Independence

Global Trader does not run any internal trading risk and therefore offers completely unbiased execution.

Anonymity

Global Trader routes all transactions anonymously through electronic gateways directly to the exchanges, ensuring 'no name give up' for individual orders. Trades vulnerability for opportunity.

Direct Market Access

Global Trader provides a single access point to over 90% of the world's equity market liquidity through a single trading screen.

Straight through processing

Global Trader provides straight-through-processing from order entry to trade confirmation.

Shrinking the world

Global Trader shrinks the world for your convenience. It services clients in 29 countries from its offices in London, Johannesburg, Cape Town, Toronto, Moscow and Bangkok.

Fully regulated

Global Trader is authorised and regulated by the Financial Services Authority of the United Kingdom and the Guernsey Financial Services Commission.

Global Trader is registered as a derivatives dealer with the Securities and Exchange

Commission of Thailand, a member of the London Stock Exchange and a derivative member of the Johannesburg Stock Exchange in South Africa.

World-class partners

Global Trader facilitates client transactions via relationships with tier one hedging counterparties

- ING
- UBS
- Calyon
- Bear Sterns
- Jeffries
- Dresdner Kleinwort

Global Trader is different because we offer:

- Tier 1 assurance
- Unparalleled market coverage*
- Emerging market specialisation
- Boutique house service levels
- Advanced DMA trading systems
- Real-time trade and historic position reporting
- Algorithmic trading capabilities
- Superior flexibility and operational efficiency including post-trade allocation
- Institution grade volume trading capacity and straight-through processing
- Trade give-ups from other brokers
- Advanced order and execution management tools including trailing orders, iceberg and single-ticket entry

*The markets we offer:

Europe: UK, Denmark, France, Germany, Greece, Hungary, Ireland, Italy, Netherlands, Norway, Poland, Romania, Russia, Russia ADR/GDR, Sweden, Bulgaria, Czech Republic, Switzerland.

Asia: Taiwan, Thailand, Hong Kong, Indonesia, Japan, Korea, Malaysia, Singapore.

The rest of the world: USA, Canada, South Africa, Australia.

If you would like to know more please visit **www.gt247.com** or call **020 7420 1200**.

CFDs are only suitable for investors with sufficient experience and knowledge. Experienced private investors will be opted up to intermediate customer classification pursuant to the rules of the Financial Services Authority of the United Kingdom.

Risk Warning

CFDs carry a high level of risk to your capital. Only speculate with money you can afford to lose as you may lose more than your original deposit. CFDs can be very volatile and prices may move rapidly against you. Resulting losses may require further payments to be made. CFDs may not be suitable for all customers, so ensure you fully understand the risks involved and seek independent advice if necessary.

initial margin required. The margin is on the high side for stocks outside the FTSE-100, and on the low side for indices.

If you have a long position in a stock, you will have to pay a financing charge. This may be, for instance, LIBOR (London Interbank Offered Rate), defined on Day 16, plus 1.5 per cent – for the outstanding amount above the margin. The rate payable is pro rata to the annual rate. If you have a short position, you will similarly be paid financing (perhaps LIBOR – 2.5 per cent) for this. If you close out your CFD intraday, financing payments will not apply, as for rolling online spread bets (again, see Day 16).

The CFD has no settlement date, unlike for futures and spread betting where the contract on expiry must be rolled over to the next one. As in spread betting, you will pay no stamp duty on your CFD purchase but, after you have held it for about 60 days, the amount that you saved this way compared with on shares is cancelled by your interest payments. From this time, it makes no economic sense to continue holding your CFD unless it is significantly increasing in value.

Unlike in spread betting, you are liable for capital gains tax on profits beyond your annual exemption level (£8,500 in 2006–7), and you may offset losses against future liabilities.

Foreign exchange

An accessible market

Foreign exchange (forex) is the most liquid of the margin products, and London has the largest market in the world, partly because it is well positioned in the global time zones. Forex is a 24-hour market, which means a dramatic move can take place when you are in bed at night. You can protect yourself against any adverse consequences by using a limit order (discussed on Day 14), which enables you to trade at a predetermined level. You may also take out a stop loss.

As a speculator, you will buy or sell one currency against another, and foreign exchange can be a way to diversify your portfolio. You may also hedge. If you bought a cottage in Italy for £100,000, and are worried that the value in sterling may fall after a couple of years, you can use the currency market to hedge against euro depreciation. International companies may hedge to protect against the differential between the currency in which they report earnings and that in which they pay dividends.

If you trade forex directly, the bid–offer spread is very tight and, as a private investor, you can trade on the same terms as institutions, which was not the case a few years ago.

Most of your trading will probably be in the three largest markets: euro/dollar, dollar/yen and sterling/dollar, also known as the *cable* rate. At the time of preparing this edition of the book, some forex speculators have made significant money on the weakening dollar.

Unlike shares, currencies are not linked to underlying value. They do not reflect, for instance, director sales or profit warnings. But they can swing as a result of unexpected interest rate figures.

When you trade in forex, as in derivatives, you make money only from volatility. It tends to be high even on quiet days, and traders have found it profitable to go *with* the flow. David Jones, chief market analyst at CMC Markets, has described forex as a market that 'plays by the rules of technical analysis' (see Days 8, 9 and 10).

You may follow major currency values in one column in your newspaper. The arrival of the euro has made the market smaller and so made your job easier.

Trading outlets

In forex, you may trade either physical money, or derivatives. Let us look at each.

Forex brokers will trade directly for you, but may require evidence that you have some trading experience. As with derivatives, you will pay initial margin, in the form of upfront cash, which you need to top up where needed, failing which the broker will close your open position at a loss. Your position in forex is commonly leveraged by up to several hundred times, which is much more than in derivatives.

To reduce pricing unpredictability, find a broker that will trade at the price on the screen, known as the *dealable* rate. You may have to pay a commission, percentage based or fixed, on trading. Look for a good value package.

Your easiest way to gain access to foreign exchange derivatives is through spread betting or CFDs, where the spreads can be as competitive as those available to institutions spot trading forex directly. Forex options are over the counter and mainly for institutions. The futures market is on-exchange is for experienced investors.

Training

Some dealers, including GNI Touch (www.gnitouch.com) and CMC Markets (www.cmcmarkets.co.uk), offer free training sessions. Many firms offer facilities for placing mock trades.

The way forward

This concludes our look at CFDs and forex, and derivatives in general. In Part 5, we will take a broader look at the City.

Dynamic rules

- ■ CFDs give you exposure to price movement in the underlying instrument without buying it.
- ■ More than 20 per cent of trading volume on the London Stock Exchange is on CFDs.
- ■ You can trade CFDs through spread betting firms. Alternatively, you may use brokers, where costs can be lower but the minimum deal size is larger.
- ■ Institutional investors trade CFDs and spread betting firms sometimes use them to lay off their own bets.
- ■ There is no stamp duty on your purchase of CFDs, but the saving you make compared with on shares is wiped out by interest payments if you hold for longer than about 60 days.
- ■ Foreign exchange is traded 24 hours a day and London has the largest market.
- ■ The three largest forex markets are euro/dollar, dollar/yen and sterling/dollar (cable).
- ■ You can trade currencies in physical money, or through derivatives.

Part 5

The Broader Picture

Media and publicity power

Overview

In this module, we will look at the hidden world of public relations, and how journalists and share tipsters work. We will focus on how companies distribute price-sensitive information. We will take a look at online bulletin boards and the high-margin business of investment seminars.

The hidden hand of public relations

Many a share tip started life as the creation of a public relations (PR) agency. Let us shine a torch on the dark and well-paid art of PR. The agencies construct an image for quoted companies to impress on financial journalists and, in so far as they will listen, analysts. They play a major part in distributing company results, which, based on a 31 December year-end, are published in March and September.

To the initiated eye, the unseen hand of PR is discernible every day in the press. The large agencies are linked with main City activity, and the many other agencies pick up the smaller jobs. Journalists tend to depend on PR executives, finding them more willing to explain basics than company executives.

The press

Financial journalism, cynics have said, is a last refuge of scoundrels. It attracts men and women from all walks of life and is a branch of the trade that, unlike local newspaper journalism for instance, has no recognized qualifications.

Of the many wise and wonderful things that are said about journalists, one is that their role has 'power without responsibility', and another is that 'you cannot bribe the British journalist'. Both of these sayings have enough truth to have made them part of our culture but neither tells the full story. Let us take a look at how members of the financial press ply their trade.

The journalists create stories from basic information in a news release and may use some of it verbatim. The release may convey a slanted message. If a company's sales are up but its profits are down, the release may put the emphasis on the sales. If net profits are down but pre-tax profits are up, it may highlight the latter. Journalists often do not read between the lines. This can be due to a lack of accounting knowledge, or plain laziness.

Some resent the industry that they write about because it pays its front-line performers so much more than they earn. They may relish opportunities to put the boot in, and make good use of information leaks from bankers and stockbrokers perhaps anxious to scupper the business of their rivals. They will print the one-sided story if it checks out enough to avoid libel risk.

National newspapers are more careful and more balanced in their reporting than some of the trade press, but may also go into less depth. Jason Nissé wrote in *The Independent* on 14 May 2006, shortly before being lured away from his post there as business editor to become public relations director at Barclays:

> An investment banker once said to me that the problem with journalists is that they only ever know about a third of the story at best. Soon I will know whether this was a cruel indictment of my career so far – or a tellingly accurate comment.

The company perspective

Quoted companies use public relations resources and the press to communicate with investors in a way that avoids creating, or continuing, a false market in the shares.

A company with price-sensitive information will initially release it through a Regulatory Information Service to ensure equal access. RNS is the largest such service and it disseminates more than 500 announcements every business day. You may access it through the website of its provider, the London Stock Exchange, at www.londonstockexchange.com. When inside information is distributed at a meeting, an announcement must be made immediately, or have been made in advance.

Companies must disclose significant transactions, or those by related parties, such as directors. To keep the market informed about the likely end-of-year results and to avoid a false market, they may make announcements more often than is required. The information disclosed should be complete.

Market abuse, including insider dealing, leading to only small price movements, may not attract regulatory attention because the Financial Services Authority (FSA) reacts proportionately to the risk, according to lawyers.

Tip sheets

Tip sheets provide share recommendations to investors. They can attract a loyal following but may not be perceptive or well informed. Tipsters may write columns for newspapers and trade magazines as well as the newsletters, or via web-based subscription services. Some have an influence out of all proportion to their track record. The most usual background is financial journalism, which requires an ability to summarize complex arguments, but not much more.

Some tipsters will have worked in the City of London or on Wall Street, but it does not in itself add value to their recommendations. Most tipsters do not have the skill to dissect the company report and accounts but will sprinkle their recommendations with references to it. Some tipsters never invest in shares, at least separately from their tipping. The adage applies: if the tipsters know so much, why are they not investing instead of showing others how to do it?

If it is asking too much for tipsters to be the investment gurus that their promotional literature so often claims they are, it is reasonable to ask for professionalism in research and presentation. Like many journalists, tipsters are often too lazy or time-stretched to develop useful contacts and to produce independent work. Some rely mainly on secondary sources. Such a tipster lifts stories from newspapers, other tip sheets, and the bulletin boards on financial websites – places to which everybody has access – and amalgamates them. The tipster will pass off the result, complete with a personalized twist or two, as his or her own work.

It is not as deplorable as it sounds. As a tip sheet subscriber, you are paying for how information is packaged as much as for what it contains. But the tip needs to be sincere and it sometimes falls short. To present a credible front, the tipster will often hint at City contacts and confidential tip-offs. Another tactic is to claim the role of advocate for the man in the street, sifting through the City jargon and subterfuge. One tip sheet editor claims to write his tip sheet in the language people use in his local pub.

If a tipster wants to keep his or her reputation intact, it can pay not to be associated with one website or newsletter for too long, as its tipping record will at some point go through a lean period. For this reason, newsletter writers are often willing to move jobs or work for several publications at once. As an alternative strategy, they try to develop a high-profile name and to build up a following by infusing personality into their writing.

Whatever the approach, the secret of successful tipping from the business perspective is to write convincingly, perhaps entertainingly, while presenting an image of authority and expertise. It is *not* based on how many of the recommendations turn out well. When a small company tip is given prominence in a popular newsletter, as tends to happen, the market makers increase the price. Other tipsters get wind and steal the idea. It is a vicious circle which can send the share price up temporarily.

Tip sheet subscribers understand the game and it is better that they do so. Interactive Investor once asked its site visitors whether they agreed that some named tipsters had tipped one too many duds. A staggering 80.39 per cent of respondents agreed, and only 5.94 per cent disagreed. The rest did not know. Note this online comment about one of the tipsters:

> The fundamentals are right, he always says of shares he recommends... his arrogance kept people hanging in when they [the shares] were falling... and so many people trusted him and paid him for what they thought was his competence ... Be ashamed [tipster]... you couldn't even help people get out ... I've lost a lot of money.

Subscribers usually come back for more. Greed is a powerful emotion and promoters feed it by suggesting that tip sheets can make subscribers a lot of money. The FSA's recent crackdown on dubious financial promotions has made tip sheet promoters more careful about how they convey this message but there are methods that have stood the test of time. Some tip sheets promise to return your subscription fee if at least several of their tips have not doubled in the year but may make so many tips that the forfeit never arises.

Be particularly wary about newspaper tips. The journalists will often have received their tips from a PR consultant pushing the company. They are publishing it to return a favour as well as, of course, to fill up space. They do not really know about the value of their tip, and do not care. The game is less manipulative than it was. Until fairly recently, some PR agents leaked price-sensitive information to newspapers with impunity, but regulations have caught up.

In early 2006, two financial journalists were successfully prosecuted by the Department of Trade and Industry for having bought shares ahead of tipping them in a national newspaper and selling out after publication when the tip had pushed up the share price.

The famous *Friday night drop* where PR agents would queue to give stories to Sunday newspaper journalists no longer exists.

My concluding advice is to take most tipsters with a pinch of salt. They can sometimes point you in the direction of interesting companies, but tips must be an adjunct to, and not a substitute for, your own research.

A selection of tip sheets

Most newsletters offer trial subscriptions or free copies. Always take up the offer, and see how the tips turn out before you subscribe. I like the tip sheet *t1ps.com* (www.t1ps.com), written by Tom Winnifrith, which selects stocks based largely on fundamentals. I enjoy *Red Hot Penny Shares* from Fleet Street Publications (www.fleetstreetpublications.co.uk). I value *Techninvest* (www. techinvest.ie), a tip sheet which focuses on high-tech shares; the website offers you a free sample edition.

A useful source of small company tips is *Growth Company Investor* (www. growthcompany.co.uk). An interesting tip sheet is *Trendwatch* (www.trend-watch.co.uk), where recommendations are based on software identification of share price trends. Gain access to offbeat share tips, rumours and educational material as well as share tips at Share Crazy (www.sharecrazy.com).

Small company investors may want to visit the tipping website of former *Daily Mail* journalist Michael Walters (www.michaelwalters.com). As newspaper share tipsters go, he was one of the greats.

Some newsletter writers have turned themselves into the stuff of legend through self-publicity campaigns across continents. Among these is Chevalier Harry D (for Dynamic) Schultz, KHC, KM, KCPR, KCSA, KCSS. To set the tone, Schultz, who as this second edition goes to press is in his seventies, reminds people via his website that he has been the highest paid investment consultant in the world at US~$2,400 per hour, or US~$3,400 at weekends (international edition, *Guinness Book of Records 1981–2000*). I once met Schultz at an investment conference in Monte Carlo and found him a friendly fellow.

The International Harry Shultz Letter (www.hsletter.com) is based in Switzerland and has subscribers in 71 nations. It is written in abbreviated prose (U instead of you), with a good sense of humour. The Letter is based on libertarian views, has a US flavour and heavy leanings towards technical analysis. It is not everybody's cup of tea. Over the more than 40 years of its life, the Letter has not always had a good track record, as investment writer John Train has publicly observed. But the Letter has loyal subscribers. Schultz displays on his website this excerpt from what he calls a super e-mail with a great punch line: 'Thanx for paying attention to your clients. Some of us know how U helped us preserve our nest egg of retirement monies and its purchasing power. Soooo, U see, there is Uncle Sam – who takes, and Uncle Harry – who gives.'

Harry Schultz has links with the world of unconventional tax avoidance techniques. For all but a few, this is a bit of a fantasy. To get the flavour, visit the website of Eden Press, a California-based alternative tax haven information bookseller, at www.edenpress.com.

Internet bulletin boards

Useful as they are, the internet bulletin boards are unreliable. Some contributors are sincere, but their quality of input will vary. Many aim to influence trading of the stock by others so that they or their paymasters can buy or sell at a more congenial price.

Using several aliases, they may refer repeatedly to news that adversely affects the company, and has at least some truth. By criticizing a stock little and often through the bulletin boards, they cast doubt on it. There is some truth in their comments, which lends plausibility, but in areas where you cannot easily check, they will mix in lies.

Once, a fund manager made misleading comments about a company on the bulletin boards of a major financial news site and, to his surprise, the company tracked him down and took legal action. The matter was settled out of court. This gave some financial websites a fright and some started monitoring the bulletin boards more carefully. But traders who post dubious messages anonymously and from internet cafés cannot be traced, and many are wise to this.

When you use the internet bulletin boards, you will come across the manipulators. Do not argue or reason with them. You would not only be wasting your time, but would give them attention they can exploit. Focus instead on messages from those who post occasionally but seem to have something to say. Check any potentially significant matters raised with the company itself or a sector analyst.

Training and seminars

Starting traders ask me to recommend and, increasingly, to run seminars on trading. It never ceases to amaze me how many online requests I receive. The inquirers have in common that they are well educated but not very experienced at trading and they are willing to invest significant money in gaining the magic touch from a guru. I tell them the game does not work like that. I advise them to go away and do some low-level trading themselves for six months or a year, practising money management (see Day 14). They may consult books like this one, which is not going to break the bank.

If the trader then still wants expensive training, he or she will be more ready. There are some esoteric training programmes on offer, including based on – wait for it – astrology, whose most famous user, albeit on a closet basis, was trader William G Gann. Even nonsensical trading systems can work if, alongside their selection criteria, they require standard money management techniques, including cutting losses and running profits. I know of one trader who used astrology to trade successfully, as it seemed to me, because of that discipline.

Most training for traders is more on the conventional side. It focuses on money management, charting, and deploying a range of financial instruments, particularly derivatives. There is no shortage of self-proclaimed experts who will take your shilling. But any who make money as traders are, for obvious reasons, thin on the ground.

The seminar business does not have a register of approved persons like for brokers. I know of some real rogues who have jumped onto the training bandwagon, including one fresh out of jail for securities theft.

The free seminars run by firms are often the most insidious. They tend to promote technical analysis in too simplistic a way and may encourage frequent trading, which often benefits nobody but the broker. I know of firms that bribe delegates at free seminars to sign up as clients.

Other seminars are simply an advert for expensive software or training. I know of one individual who places huge adverts for a free course regularly in the national press. The course, run from a hired hotel room, is a pack of lies designed to suggest that it is easy to make huge profits on the stock market, and, at the end, most of those present are persuaded to get out their credit cards and pay for an expensive follow-up course. You have every right to spend your money on such showmanship but, please, do it with your eyes open. See Day 16 for my warnings about dubious spread betting training.

The way forward

The media plays a significant part in promoting the stock market as well as exposing it. Either way, what it serves up is probably not the whole story.

Dynamic rules

■ The PR agencies seek to control the agenda of journalists.

■ Even the best journalists may run with only part of a story.

■ A company will initially release price-sensitive information through a regulatory information service to ensure equal access.

■ Share tipsters are rarely skilled at stock picking. Use their ideas, if at all, as a starting point for your own research.

■ The internet bulletin boards are largely unregulated, and are used by many contributors with a vested interest. They can be helpful in flagging issues of concern, but check the facts with a reliable source, ideally the underlying company.

■ Avoid expensive trading seminars when you are starting out. You can get the theory cheaply from books, and from a practical point of view, there is no substitute for your own trading efforts.

Sharp operators at work

Overview

This module is about how dubious stockbrokers and other financial advisers work. They are in a minority, but they target inexperienced investors. This short module will help you to steer clear.

Unauthorized firms

The boiler rooms

The boiler rooms operate both online and by telephone, typically from abroad. They are unauthorized by the Financial Services Authority. Their websites are slick and bold. They provide a phone number as well as an e-mail address, but a telephone approach will reach only an answer phone.

The promoter claims to be a broker or a bank, depending on which type of scam it is trying to pull off. Its name may sound like that of a big-name financial institution, giving it a ring of familiarity that will strike a chord with the gullible. Some of the fraudulent internet banks have claimed to be based in Jersey, Guernsey, or the Isle of Man, at street addresses that do not exist, much to the exasperation of local regulators.

The dubious brokers are expert at hard-selling shares in unknown companies, which, if they exist at all, are probably not generating revenue. The telesales people working for the outfit have the standard characteristics of the con artist. Most live as lavishly as they can, and an astute few save up to buy a comfortable early retirement, but they have in common that they are not interested in giving any kind of genuine service. In closing sales of shares on the telephone, they have the knack of conveying gravitas and the right sense of urgency. The dealers convey the unseen impression that they are sitting at a dealing deck in smart business attire but, in reality, they are lounging about in T-shirt and jeans.

The salespeople represent the stock they are pushing as a hot investment opportunity. Any who are stupid enough to send money to this outfit will lose every penny. The victims tend not to learn from their mistakes.

The outfit will refer you to a website representing the company whose shares it promotes. The site paints a glowing picture of the company, no doubt using every high-tech catch phrase, but it is a work of fiction. The company's executives are given track records with named blue-chip companies and a business education at a world-class university. If you check with the organizations, you will find no record of the named individuals, but it is a hassle to do this and the fraudsters rely on you not bothering.

The telesales people are paid a commission on sales of between 10 and 60 per cent of money taken in, which is high. Once a salesperson has *opened up* a client, the lead is passed onto a loader, who proceeds to load the individual with as much stock as he or she is willing to buy, within as short a time as possible.

The stock on offer from the fraudsters is likely to be a classic pump-and-dump. This is a planned sales campaign which sends the share price artificially spiralling. The promoters will have bought shares earlier and made a huge profit from selling out high, at which point the edifice comes crashing down, leaving a vast majority of investors holding overpriced stock that they cannot easily sell.

Sometimes, the approach is not as subtle as this, but the fraudsters simply pocket the proceeds of any cheque sent in, regardless of what stock it was intended to pay for.

The crooks may represent their share-selling campaign as an IPO or private placing and invite you to subscribe early at a *special* price. The dealer may send out a prospectus. This will have some unrealistic profits and cash flow projections, and will be full of warnings. The company may have no revenues, let alone profits. But some greedy investors will not take the hint.

You will be in and out within a month, the broker may say, and promises clients a small profit – big enough to entice them, but not enough to make them suspicious. To release capital, some clients will empty their building societies and cash in investment funds. After buying the new stock, they will never be able to sell out, but it will not be immediately apparent. The broker will say clients should stay invested because of market conditions or the exchange rate.

The only market maker for the stock will be the broker who sold it. If the firm refuses to buy the stock back, it will be worthless. It *may* allow clients to sell out, only if they will reinvest in an equally dubious stock. Either way, the clients will never see the colour of their money. Before their hope is entirely shattered, the firm will push the dubious stock, and others like it, hard. It may launch *dog-and-pony* client evenings in top London hotels, and invite dupes into luxury offices for lunch.

You may ask how such a situation could be allowed to arise in the first place. An unscrupulous firm occasionally takes over a struggling but basically honest company whose good name it exploits. The new owner will stave off suspicious regulators and others as the firm rips off clients. The firm will eventually cease trading and the principals will skip the country, if they had ever been in it, leaving their highly paid management team, and probably others, to carry the can.

In dealing with these wide-boys, it is a case of *Don't ring us, we'll ring you*. They can and will reach you if you were remiss enough to give them your telephone number. If you ring them, your call is likely to be diverted from a UK line to Croatia, Costa Rica, or wherever else the outfit is hiding out. Your salesperson will be using a false name, often with an English upper middle class ring. Such tactics make it hard for any suspicious or angry punters to trace the fraudsters. The jurisdiction will have been chosen because local police are not much concerned about what businesses are doing if they are not targeting nationals. If the police start investigating, the telesales team simply bolts to another jurisdiction.

Every boiler room collapses but it often re-emerges under another name like a phoenix from the ashes. Following a collapse, a secretly linked outfit may approach the victims and claim to recover the money they have invested. The catch is that it will demand an upfront fee. Many fall for what turns out to be a second scam.

Other financial services scams

Share and other financial services rip-offs have the same aim and are often run by the same people. Some are still peddling the notorious Nigerian 419 fraud. It is a type of advance fee fraud, named after the section of Nigeria's penal code which addresses fraud schemes. The fraudsters will send you, the potential victim, an e-mail, typically but not invariably purporting to be from a Nigerian, which contains an ungrammatical but pedantically polite plea for help. The writer appears uneducated, a ploy designed to lower your guard. The request is to make temporary use of your bank account to deposit large claimed government or other funds in return for a hefty percentage cut.

Any who respond are asked to pay an upfront fee to release the cash, and, if they should demur, may be invited to complete the transaction in Nigeria.

If the hapless mark makes the trip, the fun and games will only have started. First, the mark will be fleeced of the *fee* and second, crooks claiming to be local police will inform the individual that it was a scam and demand a further fee to retrieve the funds. They are part of the same fraud and, if you play along, you will be throwing good money after bad. The 419 fraud is so well publicized that you should not have fallen for it in the first place. Victims are reluctant to complain because the proposition on which they had allowed themselves to enter negotiations was dubious.

If you want to know more about 419, there are plenty of websites to help you. My favourite is www.419eater.com because it publishes real-life scam-baiting correspondence, where the potential victim puts the scamster to enormous trouble and ultimately declines to part with money.

Another growing fraud is phishing, where the fraudsters trick people into revealing their bank account details and passwords, or similar sensitive information, by e-mail. They will send out e-mails that purport to be from a big-name high street bank and carry something that looks like its logo. The e-mail claims it is checking accounts, and it asks for your account details and password. If you oblige, as at least a few do, the crooks will empty your account.

The victims

Some of the victims may not understand what happened. For those who do, there is nothing much they can do to retrieve money invested. Some of the wealthier victims may themselves be money launderers and crooks, in which case they can be relied on not to kick up a fuss about their losses, at least in public. The vast majority of victims are ordinary people, with varying levels of financial resources. They have in common only that they are gullible and greedy. Even prominent businessmen can behave like children in a sweetshop.

Authorized firms

The dubious brokers

Dubious brokers and share salespeople operate today in UK authorized firms. Some are half-commission brokers, attached to stockbroking firms that pay them a percentage of commission on every trade and keep the rest of it. Others are salaried. The firms may have a history of surviving regulatory action and fines. They may sell speculative shares to private investors, but, unlike some continental bucket shops, will not usually steal money outright.

Some of the dubious individuals will have been trained at licensed dealers in securities authorized by the Department of Trade and Industry, a type of firm which was phased out with the implementation of the Financial Services Act, 1986. They will have been taught never to say that a stock *will*, or is *certain to*, rise in value. Instead, they were required to say that the stock *should*, or is *likely to*, rise in value. This way, victims of their sales pitch found it harder to accuse them of having given misleading information, particularly if the firm taped client calls.

The dubious broker presents news and research selectively to back his or her sales case. If a stock has performed poorly and has a low P/E ratio (see Day 7), the broker will say that it is undervalued, and cite studies showing that companies with low P/E ratios have historically outperformed the market. He or she will not point out that a low P/E ratio can warn of poor prospects.

Conversely, if the broker is selling a growth stock with a high P/E ratio, he or she will stress the benefits of relative strength (against the market index) and gloss over the likely overvaluation against fundamentals.

The client makes the investment decision more on the broker's telephone manner and tone of voice than on the literal meaning of his or her words. On closing the sale, the broker may cover himself or herself (perhaps for the benefit of the tape) by saying something like: 'Of course, I can't make any guarantees about any stock – you understand that?' and pause for the client's consent, before continuing with: 'With that proviso, I have great hopes for this one...'

Dubious brokers cannot always answer simple questions on the telephone and may cover up. The broker may say something like: 'Hang on please, I've just got a call coming in from the States' and will put the client on hold while he or she checks the query with somebody more knowledgeable. The broker will pick up the telephone conversation again with: 'Sorry about that. What was your question?' The client will repeat it, and the broker will provide the answer as if spontaneously.

Another tactic is to evade the question altogether. If a client asks why corporate earnings fell, the broker may parry with: 'That's unimportant for the company at this stage. What counts is revenue.' The dubious advisory broker prefers you not to sell, unless you are simultaneously reinvesting the money with him. I know of one broker who responds to client sell requests with: 'You must be out of your mind. You should be buying more.' The broker may say: 'Don't sell *that* one', implying that he or she knows of major developments within the company, but cannot reveal them.

If you prove insistent on selling, the shyster may ask you to wait for just another couple of weeks – during which, he or she implies, the company's fortunes may take a turn for the better: 'If you then still wish to sell, go ahead.' If you agree, the broker knows that there is a good chance that by then you will have more pressing priorities than selling the stock. As an added disincentive, the broker may put the onus on *you* to ring up about selling the stock. If you call, the broker may be unavailable.

The dubious salespeople will *churn* your portfolio, which is to trade with the sole aim of generating commission. Churning is not allowed, but it goes on and it cannot always be proved. The broker manipulates the private investor into making what he or she thinks is a personal decision to sell part of the portfolio and use the proceeds to buy new shares. The sales pitch will be something like: 'This small high-tech stock has never been at such a low price. That's why a lot of City professionals are quietly buying it up. Of course I couldn't *recommend* that you sell your blue-chip shares to get involved in what is technically a speculative investment. I know what I would do in your shoes but you must make your own decision.'

On such prompting, 8 clients out of 10 will sell good stocks to reinvest in speculative rubbish. Just before executing the trade, the broker will reiterate, for the benefit of the tape, that the decision is the client's and that there is a risk involved.

If you bought shares in a high-tech company, the broker will later suggest that its technology has become outdated, and will prompt you to sell the stock and reinvest elsewhere. You may be advised to sell your shares in a wire-line telephone company and reinvest in a cable technology company, then to jump ship for fibre optics. There is always a *newer* technology on the horizon.

Access to client lists

Dubious financial services promoters work the company shareholder registers. I know of one half-commission broker who gained all his clients this way. He would publish a research report on a small quoted penny stock which he gave free to interested names on its share register, and he later hit the lucky recipients with new penny share recommendations. The continental boiler rooms do the same but the stocks they sell are duds.

Legislation is threatening to make misuse of the share registers difficult. The Company Law Reform Bill, pending as this second edition goes to press, will give a company the right to refer a request for its shareholder register to court. If the court is satisfied that the register will not be used for a proper purpose, it will direct that the company need not comply with the request.

The Financial Services Authority (FSA) has said that this legislative development will make it harder for boiler rooms to continue fleecing UK investors, but will not eliminate it. The boiler rooms have *sucker* lists, made up of those who have already bought dud stocks, which they sell to each other, a spokesman for the regulator notes.

Regulatory warnings and legislation

You can check whether a company selling shares to UK investors is authorized by the FSA by visiting the regulator's website at www.fsa.gov.uk/consumer/fcs/index.html, or calling its consumer helpline on 0845 606 1234. If the share dealing firm is unauthorized, you cannot complain to the Financial Ombudsman Service or claim from the Financial Services Compensation Scheme (see Day 5 on both). Check the *Investors Chronicle* chat rooms (www.investorschronicle.co.uk) for stories of embittered investors.

The US Securities and Exchange Commission has highlighted the risks. Visit its mockup website at www.mcwhortle.com, which represents McWhortle as an 'established and well-known manufacturer of biological defense mechanisms'. Visitors are invited to apply for shares in McWhortle's IPO. They are led through to a message that reads: 'If you responded to an investment like this... You could get scammed.'

The UK government is reviewing the whole issue of fraud and in May 2005 introduced the Fraud Bill, which defines fraud for the first time in the legislation. The Bill includes new measures for modernizing the law to equip investigators and prosecutors with the tools required to keep pace with the changing world of fraud, including phishing and internet fraud, according to a Home Office statement.

The way forward

Now you have read this chapter, you know what to avoid. Do not become one of the many thousands who have assumed the role of constant victims to the sharp operators.

Dynamic rules

■ The boiler rooms sell shares in worthless stocks on the telephone. If you give them your money, you can expect to lose it.

■ The crooked brokers operate under false names and at a secret location. If trouble hits, they move their outfit elsewhere and restart under new names.

■ The Nigerian 419 and other advanced fee scams are still rife over the internet.

■ Phishing is when you are asked to give your bank details to a fraudster masquerading as a big-name bank.

- Dubious brokers may be authorized. They aim to sell you as much stock as possible, regardless of whether it is in your interests.
- Firms can buy share registers to get your name and try to sell you stocks. Pending legislation may make this more difficult for the boiler rooms.
- Check with the Financial Services Authority whether a company selling shares to UK investors is authorized.

Rich dividends from reading

Overview

Read the right investment books and it may help you to become rich, provided that you put their advice into practice. In this module, I will recommend some titles.

The online advantage

Some investment books contain the experience and wisdom of great stock market traders. One good idea can more than repay the book's cover price, and, more importantly, your time invested in reading it.

Thanks to the internet, finding out about and ordering books has never been easier. Online, you can look up individual titles, browse, read reviews and place orders for instant delivery. You may select from far more titles than are available in most bookshops.

If you buy from Global-investor.com (www.global-investor.com), my favourite bookshop, the price is often discounted and delivery is prompt and reliable. Amazon (www.amazon.co.uk) is also a useful source of business books, and publishes some sample extracts. Both of these online bookshops publish online reviews, but watch for bias.

Recommended books

I have focused my recommendations on a few books among those I have valued enough to read more than once and are not too technical. I believe they will take you forward as an investor.

Fundamental investing

One Up on Wall Street

One Up on Wall Street by Peter Lynch (Penguin Books) is the easiest and most entertaining of the investment classics that you will read. It is from a US perspective, but the wisdom is transferable. The author uses his experience as a master fund manager who worked at Fidelity to tell private investors how they can use what they know to profit from the stock market.

The book starts with an autobiographical account of how Lynch became a great stock picker, and his opening words are: 'There's no such thing as a hereditary knack for picking stocks.' Lynch notes that his college professors believed in quantum analysis and random walk and they were not doing so well as his colleagues at Fidelity where he did summer jobs.

But fund managers are too cautious to invest in spectacular growth stocks, according to Lynch. He says that private investors have greater freedom but should put the priority on owning their own house, and should only invest on the stock market what they can afford to lose.

The thrust of the book is that investors may use their own life experience to notice businesses and products which are working spectacularly well. Lynch says that you'll get your biggest moves in small companies, and that his favourite investments include small aggressive new enterprises that grow at 20 to 25 per cent a year. He discusses investing in cyclicals, turnarounds and asset plays, and seeks to define the perfect stock – with such criteria as a dull-sounding company with a niche, not owned by institutions or followed by analysts. He avoids hyped companies and those that make foolish acquisitions.

Stocks are compared to people: librarians and schoolteachers are slow growers; farmers and resort employees are cyclicals; drifters and bankrupts are turnarounds; and actors and athletes are fast growers.

Lynch warns readers to avoid stocks with excessively high P/E ratios, saying the company must have incredible earnings growth to justify the price. The book explains how to get the most out of your broker, and to call the company in which you are investing with your questions. Lynch explains how to get something out of a company report and accounts in a few minutes. He says that the real issue over dividends is how they affect the value of a company and the stock price over time.

The author examines the importance of the company's cash position, and how stated book value often bears little relationship to value. He recommends rechecking the story for companies in which you have invested, and looks at the 12 silliest things people say about stocks.

Buffettology

Buffettology by Mary Buffett and David Clark (Pocket Books) is a comprehensive book about US investor Warren Buffett's system of value investing. The authors are Mary Buffett, who initiated the book project after divorcing from Warren's son Peter, and David Clark, a portfolio analyst.

The authors say that other people's folly and Warren Buffett's discipline are the key elements of the master's investment philosophy. They note that Buffett commits capital to investment only when it makes sense from a business perspective and he prefers to acquire 100 per cent ownership of the right business or, failing that, to make a long-term minority investment in the company's common stock.

Warren Buffett puts a future value on the business using the projected compound annual rate of return, the authors note. To determine that value, Buffett requires some predictability of future earnings, a sign of *excellent* business economics.

The business economics are shown in high returns on shareholder equity, strong earnings, a consumer monopoly, and management that keep shareholders' interests in mind, according to the authors. Buffett chooses the kind of business he would like to be in, and lets the price of the security, and so the expected rate of return, decide the buy decision. The authors say that to get rich, like Buffett, you only have to earn consistently above-average annual rates of return over the long term.

The book explains how Buffett learnt from Benjamin Graham, the pioneer value investor, and from others such as Philip Fisher and Lord John Maynard Keynes. It takes you through the practical process of discounting to present value and even recommends a calculator that will do the work for you.

Buffett's thinking is that if price is the most important factor to buy, you are probably dealing with a commodity-type business, and it will give you, at best, only average long-term results. Winning companies have a consumer monopoly, where there is greater pricing flexibility because there is no effective competition.

The book explains Buffett's view that the company's franchise is more important than quality of management, but that managers should be honest. In the right company, a downturn can be an investment opportunity, and diversification is what people do to protect themselves against stupidity, according to Buffett. He tends never to sell his investments. The second half of the book focuses on the maths required to decide whether a stock's market price makes business sense.

Investing with Anthony Bolton

Investing with Anthony Bolton by Jonathan Davis (Harriman House) is a waffle-free sketch of fund manager Anthony Bolton and his investing methods, livened up with photographs. As manager of Fidelity's outperforming Special Situations fund for 24 years, Bolton attributes his success to, among other things, contrarianism, breadth of information sources, liaison with company managers, and applying the P/E ratio (see Day 7). The price at which he bought is irrelevant to trading decisions.

Bolton admires Warren Buffett but he does not similarly rely on buy and hold, according to Davis. Bolton was inspired partly by reading about such gurus but, as a young man, he had to be kicked out of bed by his father to look for a job. Bolton is not always confident in his investment decisions, and has made mistakes from investing in companies with a weak balance sheet.

The book shows how Bolton stands by his own judgement in running a portfolio with short-term volatility, the price for outperforming the market in the long term. The proof of Bolton's success lies in the performance statistics, included in the appendix. Employer Fidelity emerges as the broad-minded facilitator that took risks but Bolton is the star.

Super Stocks

Super Stocks by Kenneth L Fisher (Irwin Professional Publishing) was published in 1984 and still speaks to us. The author is the son of the late Philip A Fisher, a titan of stock market investing. Fisher uses the price/sales ratio (see Day 11), which he prefers to the P/E ratio, and the price/research ratio, to value stocks as well as to cross-check technology valuations.

The book's case is that super stocks must meet the specified criteria, including a low price/sales ratio. They must rise between 3 and 10 times in value within three to five years of purchase and offer long-term rates of return of between 25 and 100 per cent a year.

The book explains how to analyse future profit margins, a last step in deciding whether you have a super company. Investors should buy a super stock when the financial community believes it is a real dog and must forgive the management for its mistakes, according to Fisher.

The right time to sell the stock is only when its price/sales ratio gets outrageously high or it starts to fall short of the qualifying criteria for super status, according to Fisher.

Economics

The Investor's Guide to Economic Fundamentals

The Investor's Guide to Economic Fundamentals by John Calverley (John Wiley) is the best easy book on economics for investors I have ever come across. It is understandable and non-mathematical without talking down to the reader.

The author is chief economist and strategist at American Express Bank and, as may be expected, the book relates economics to investing. The focus is pan-European and reader can either dip into this text or read it from start to finish.

Calverley examines key market fundamentals such as interest rates, inflation and the business cycle and how they impact on the main areas of investment, including shares, bonds, commodities, currencies, property, emerging markets and money markets. The author advises on how to predict and manage market risk, and to allocate assets under different market conditions.

The book breaks down the key statistics (see Day 7) and explains how to interpret them and the context. Let us look at Part 1. In Chapter 1, the author defines gross domestic product, warns that its numerical precision is spurious, and explains four ways to analyse it.

In Chapter 2, Calverley says that investors can either try to spot turning points in the business cycle and shift asset allocation accordingly, or can ignore the cycle.

In Chapter 3, there is a lucid discussion of inflation, including what causes it, the complications of inflation targeting, and inflation indicators such as the Consumer Price Index. Driving forces are discussed, along with the impact of a low-inflation environment and the threat of deflation.

The new economy, and whether it is myth or reality, was topical when this book was published in 2003 and is analysed in detail in Chapter 4.

Chapter 5 focuses on Central Banks, and concepts such as the yield curve and the Taylor rule. Monetarism, monetary policy and the exchange rate, how money is created and the Basel Accord are among areas discussed.

Chapter 6 focuses on fiscal policy and why, if it is deliberately stimulatory, it is bad for the bond market but benefits currency. In Chapter 7, there is discussion of how asset prices affect the economy. Chapter 8 covers globalization and capital flows, including why current account imbalances matter, and how a country's trade regime affects its economic performance.

Chapter 9 finds evidence of global links in, for example, stock markets, and addresses why oil prices are still important. In Chapter 10, issues of emerging economies are discussed, including the Asian crisis, the 1998 Russian crisis, and the 2001–2 Argentina crisis.

Part 2 of the book focuses on the fundamentals of major asset classes, with individual chapters dedicated to money, bond, stock, currency, commodity and property markets, as well as emerging market investments.

Part 3 has a summary and conclusions, and covers finance theory and investment styles. A final chapter, now out of date, examines how fundamentals changed in the 10 years before publication.

Technical analysis

Investor's Guide to Charting

Investor's Guide to Charting, An Analysis for the Intelligent Investor by Alistair Blair (Financial Times Prentice Hall) aims to help non-chartist investors understand what chartists do. The author, an Oxford graduate and MBA with substantial City experience, is no intellectual slouch. He puts the claims of technical analysis through the wringer.

Blair starts with an arm's-length explanation of technical analysis and how it compares with fundamental analysis, and he finds some 'points of agreement'. The author explains the concept of the trend, and says the problem with trend lines is that no sooner are they in place than they have to be redrawn. He explains head and shoulders and other patterns but concludes they can be seen only in retrospect.

In discussing moving averages, Blair says you have to find a variation that works for you and, if that sounds disingenuous, don't try charting. He says that secondary indicators are shaken rather than constructed because the contents are always the same, and it's how you shake them and where you put the mirrors that make for variety and, as with a kaleidoscope, you could go on forever.

Blair describes point-and-figure charting as a 'heroic effort to sort the wheat from the chaff'. In Blair's view, Fibonacci numbers are a *lip-smacking* version of compound interest, and Elliott-inspired analysis has been applied far more widely than originally intended, giving rise to entertaining disagreements on issues such as where waves and corrections start. Blair notes that William Gann, unlike some technical analysts, was a trader, although not a successful one.

In the second part of the book, there is a look at some real charts, with telling commentaries. Blair started the book as a sceptic and, at the end, remains one. But he gives you, the reader, a fair chance to make up your own mind.

Japanese Candlestick Charting Techniques

Japanese Candlestick Charting Techniques: A Contemporary Guide to the Ancient Investment Techniques of the Far East by Steve Nison (Prentice Hall

Press) is the classic textbook on candlestick charting patterns (see Day 8), now in a second edition. The author peppers his text with oriental proverbs and he dips into Japanese history. His book has a seductive edge.

Nison forecasts that candlesticks will eventually replace bar charts because they convey more signals. Only some of the patterns have their counterparts in Western charts. The window in candlesticks equates to the familiar gap, but there is no firm equivalent to the three white soldiers, the shooting star and the doji.

The book explains candlestick continuation and reversal patterns in detail, and admits their limitations. Candlesticks do not provide traders with price targets, but, Nison points out, they can be used in conjunction with, for instance, Western point-and-figure charts which do. He shows how candlesticks may be used with the classic Fibonacci retracements, moving averages, or oscillators such as RSI or stochastics.

We are in familiar territory for technical analysts. Nison's book is not for beginners, but it presents the broad arguments for technical analysis for their benefit, skipping those against it. There is a trading slant to the book. Nison gives concise advice about, for example, placing stop losses and preserving capital, but, alas, not the benefit of any trading experience of his own.

Ultimately the author sells his expertise, and, towards the end, his seminars and videos. The text makes no mention of top traders such as Larry Williams who use technical analysis but shy from candlesticks. Why should it? As a promotional presentation of candlesticks basics, the book is unrivalled.

The Complete Guide to Point and Figure Charting

The Complete Guide to Point and Figure Charting by Heinrich Weber and Kermit Zieg (Harriman House) stands up as a self-instruction course. The authors reduce the learning process to a series of simple steps and take you through some practical examples.

This book is suitable for beginners, for whom it sets technical analysis in a broad context, and for experienced technicians who want to branch into point-and-figure. The text concentrates on the three box reversal method, the simplest and most popular kind. The authors recommend best software. They advise on how to draw charts by hand, which gives an intimate feel.

The book contains enough repetition to reinforce what you have learnt, but no waffle. The full-colour illustrations make the text more accessible. The UK/European focus with recent examples is welcome because some of the rival books are US-focused. The worked examples are precise, with yellow highlighting to indicate trend lines and similar.

All this is from a balanced joint authorship of academic and practitioner. Point-and-figure charting (see Day 8) is not everybody's cup of tea, and its simple signals can be fallacious, but it does allow the trader to apply stop losses appropriately and I value the method's focus on uncluttered supply and demand, which is what financial market dynamics are all about.

Trading

The Naked Trader

The Naked Trader by Robbie Burns (Harriman House) is a tongue-in-cheek beginner's guide to home-based share trading written from experience and largely based around the ADVFN website (see Day 2). The author reveals how he turned losses into winnings and how making money can be fun. The book explains how the author escaped the *rat race* of full-time employment to become a successful trader. It sets the tone of the book.

Burns warns against following tips and advises traders to do their own research. He partly relies on the charts. He has some simple advice, like always to check the website of companies in which you are thinking of investing, and some traders' tales. The author keeps up with new issues through *Investors Chronicle*.

He advises against investing in stocks traded on the AIM (Alternative Investment Market), which he dubs the *Absolute Investment Mistake*. He lists the seven deadly sins of stock market investing. I have rarely been so entertained by an investment book. See the website at www.nakedtrader.co.uk.

The UK Trader's Bible

The UK Trader's Bible by Dominic Connolly (Harriman House) offers lucid coverage of markets for trading, and the London Stock Exchange trading platforms, including the SETS electronic order book and the SEAQ market making system (see Day 4). The author explains Level II systems, and how market makers and retail service providers work. He discusses trading instruments such as contracts for difference in detail.

There is a lot on trading strategies, and on capital markets, including IPOs, placings, rights issues and takeovers. The book explains event opportunities such as lock-up expiries and credit rating changes, and stock borrowing and lending. There is a large section on takeovers.

Some of the content outdates quickly, so watch the website of the London Stock Exchange (www.londonstockexchange.com) for developments.

The Disciplined Trader

The Disciplined Trader by Mark Douglas (New York Institute of Finance) offers insights into market psychology. It advises on how to think, train and act as a trader, but does not offer a specific trading system. In Parts 1 and 2, Douglas explains the importance of self-discipline in trading, and this is his most original contribution. He says that markets are fluid, in perpetual motion, and offer unlimited potential gain and loss.

In most jobs there is a trade-off between time and effort on the one hand and money earned on the other, but it does not apply to trading, according to Douglas. To succeed as a trader requires a major mental adjustment, he says.

In Part 3, the author focuses on the power of belief and how to overcome negative thoughts. Shifting into technical analysis territory, he discusses trend theory, and use of support and resistance lines. In Part 4, the author brings together the threads that make up his case. He urges you to train yourself to trade and to focus on a single trading system to the exclusion of all else, including information overload. The next stage is to think in probabilities and to take the position that 'anything can happen'.

Real traders will forgive the laborious style and repetitions, the lack of structure and overall density. The book is hypnotic. It tells you truths about trading and markets that nobody else puts into words.

Trading for a Living

Trading for a Living by Dr Alexander Elder (John Wiley) provides a detailed blueprint for starting technical traders. The author is a US-based psychiatrist born in Russia and he views share trading from the vantage point of the couch, coupled with his own market experience. Many books on trading are dully written, but this one is intriguing. It is easy to read and carefully crafted.

Elder says that successful trading stands on three pillars: psychology, market analysis and trading systems, and money management. He explains how to manage emotions as a trader, and the deficiencies of the stock market guru. The author presents several trading systems as well as his ideas about the crowd psychology of markets.

Reminiscences of a Stock Operator

Reminiscences of a Stock Operator by Edwin Lefevre (John Wiley) is a thinly disguised account of the life of legendary share trader Jesse Livermore in early 20th-century America, and demonstrates how, as a trader, you should not fight the market.

The protagonist wins at trading shares through the bucket shop brokers of his era so spectacularly that they start refusing to take his business. He declines to rely on tips, and finds that he needs to work full time at speculation to achieve success.

The hero says he would never buy stocks even in a bull market unless they behaved as they should in that kind of market. He says that to disregard the big swing and try to jump in and out of the market is fatal to him. As the book explains, to lose money is the least of his troubles but to be wrong and not taking the loss is what does damage to the pocketbook and the soul. In the protagonist's experience, the speculator's deadly enemies are ignorance, greed, fear and hope.

The book was first published in 1923 in the vernacular of the place and time. It is not the easiest of reads for the modern reader, but remains compelling and relevant. As the protagonist says, 'There is nothing new on Wall Street.' Many professionals regard this as the greatest book on stock market trading ever written.

The Next Big Investment Boom

The Next Big Investment Boom by Mark Shipman (Kogan Page) is a successful investor and consultant's advice on how to invest in the stock market and commodities. This is an easy-to-read book with a strong leaning towards technical analysis, and will help to focus any investor's mind.

Early in the book, Shipman explains how he follows the trend, waiting for the market to make a first move and then jumping on for the ride. He says no investing strategy has come close to matching the performance of a long-term trend-following strategy, and it helps him avoid the classic mistake of adding to a losing position.

He criticises the buy-and-hold investment philosophy on the grounds that it does not offer a disciplined exit rule, and offers no protection against a market collapse. In contrast, a trend-following approach can keep investors out of the market in downturns and get them back in during rallies, according to Shipman. He says that the right temperament for an investor is cold logic.

Shipman says that you should invest only cash for which you have no immediate plans, and that if you stay in underperforming assets only because they offer diversification, you will have poor returns. He prefers to *concentrate* investments in asset classes that are appreciating in value.

Shipman recommends investing only in a market where the weekly closing price is above the current 40-week moving average and the trend of that 40-week moving average is upwards. He recommends establishing a position when the current week's closing price is the highest price of the last 12 weeks, which in market terminology is an upside breakout. Shipman offers exit strategies, and, later in the book, focuses on commodities investing and spread betting, futures and commodity-based funds.

Derivatives and risk management

The Investor's Toolbox

The Investor's Toolbox: How to Use Spreadbetting, CFDs, Options, Warrants and Trackers to Boost Returns and Reduce Risk by Peter Temple (Harriman House) sets out the choice of investments available to investors for tailoring their risk more precisely and for potentially enhancing their returns. It covers options, stock futures, covered warrants, contracts for difference, exchange-traded funds and spread betting (see Days 15, 16 and 17). The author, a former City analyst, explains how the instruments work, the dealing costs, the relationship to the underlying price, and the risk.

This book enables investors to move from simple share ownership to wider opportunities. It was published in June 2003 and the products and their markets have developed since then, but the basics remain the same. The book gives you enough information to compare products.

The first chapter includes an entertaining history of derivatives, quoting from Shakespeare's *Merchant of Venice* and Charles Mackay's classic book *Extraordinary Popular Delusions and the Madness of Crowds*. The book shows you how to select suitable software and to harness the power of the internet.

Dealing with Financial Risk

Dealing with Financial Risk by David Shirreff (The Economist in conjunction with Profile Books) is an easy-to-read introduction to risk management. For the serious learner, the book skims over detail. For the reader in a hurry, it is the perfect overview.

The tone is set by the warning that derivatives 'cannot come with enough health warnings'. The author says that the Black–Scholes model (see Day 15), used sometimes to value derivatives, is only as good as the assumptions fed into it.

Risk managers are split between those who rely on such models and those who don't, and the author concludes that humans constantly fail to predict behaviour. He sees the swap as a 'sleight of hand' and the unbundling of risks as impossible.

The author finds that financial regulators are concerned more for the health of the system than about individual banks. He says regulation will be simplified only after regulators find they have spent two decades going up a blind alley. In the second part of the book, the author provides case studies of where risk management went wrong.

Investment banking and capital markets

The Penguin Guide to Finance

The Penguin Guide to Finance by Hugo Dixon (Penguin Books) explains corporate finance and financial markets in layman's terms and has entertaining fictionalized examples. The book is rooted in seminars the author gave to journalists while he was head of Lex at the *Financial Times* and to non-specialists elsewhere. The tools of analysis used in the City and on Wall Street are covered along with the accepted wisdom of the business schools and economics faculties. The author reveals his own shortcut analytical techniques.

The book is in five parts: the foundations of finance, including the time value of money, capital markets and cost of capital; valuing companies, starting with making the distinction between profit and cash flow; how companies can increase their values, with a focus on such financial tools as gearing, mergers, acquisitions, and break-ups; financial markets and how they are valued in their entirety; and financial pathology, including irrational investment behaviour.

Monkey Business

Monkey Business: Swinging Through the Wall Street Jungle by John Rolfe and Peter Troobe (Warner Business Books) is an entertaining assault on the values of investment banking, based partly on the authors' experience of working at a named investment bank. The authors recall a story in the press of how a managing director dropped his pants and defecated in the first class cabin of an airplane, and they say it gives an understanding of what bankers do: consume, process and disseminate. High compensation is in place for investment bankers because the job sucks, the authors say.

The ideal analyst is someone with above-average intelligence, a love of money, a view of the world conforming with that of the Marquis de Sade, and the willingness to work all night, every night, with a big grin on his face, like the joker from *Batman*, the book says. The authors describe other investment banking roles in similarly unflattering terms.

The authors expose dubious valuation methods, and describe discounted cash flow analysis as the 'granddaddy of all crocks of shit', and particularly useful for valuing companies with no real business. Here is a broadly accurate picture of investment banking, at least during bull markets. It gives the book an uneasy educational value.

The Real Cost of Capital

The Real Cost of Capital by Tim Ogier, John Rugman and Lucinda Spicer (Financial Times Prentice Hall) is an easy and stimulating introduction to measuring cost of capital. The authors, a team of three at PricewaterhouseCoopers, give the Capital Asset Pricing Model (see Day 7) the significant priority it has earned in the real world, but warn of its deficiencies.

They compare historical betas, used in the model, to a traffic cop pointing a speed gun at cars, but with only a ±20 per cent accuracy tolerance, and with six ways of calculating speed, each valid but having a different result – used to assess a car that is not there.

The guidance on estimating the international weighted average cost of capital – using mainly versions of CAPM – breaks new ground. The authors consider whether a business can raise capital more cheaply in one market than another.

There is a refreshing assault on DCF forecasts, for which cost of capital is used as a key interest rate. The book explores real options valuation, no longer used much, as an alternative.

Chapter summaries reinforce points and hypothetical case studies bring practical issues to the forefront. Questions posed at the start of the book are answered at the end.

The City and financial news

Finally, here are two of my own books, which I have included not least because they are more up to date than their competitors. Both books tap deep into City sources and I suggest they may prove a worthwhile investment. Let us take a look at each.

The Times: How to Understand the Financial Pages

The Times: How to Understand the Financial Pages by Alexander Davidson (Kogan Page) is a book in two parts. Part 1 guides you through the business and money pages of *The Times*, explaining what the statistics mean, how to understand the share price tables and how to calculate the key ratios. The section gives you enough whirlwind explanations of economics and how the City works to make sense of business news and inflation indicators.

The second half of this book is an A–Z encyclopaedia that covers the background that you need to understand every area of the financial press. It explains such concepts as discounted cash flow analysis and the Capital Asset Pricing Model, and instructs on how to read company reports and accounts using International Financial Reporting Standards, which are now compulsory for UK listed companies. The book discusses every main type of financial instrument. It explains how the main City institutions work.

The role of analysts comes under scrutiny. Key ratios are explained. The book has comprehensive coverage of technical analysis, and accompanying charts. The book offers extensive information and its ordered structure and indexing give it value as both a reference source and a straight read.

The Times: How the City Really Works

The Times: How the City Really Works by Alexander Davidson (Kogan Page) is designed to be read straight through, and it aims to give you a good grounding in how parts of the City are interconnected, and how they work. The book focuses on the international nature of the City and how the UK is implementing European legislation, sometimes in conflict with the Financial Services Authority's principles-based regime.

You will find here explanations of all the main products, including equities, bonds, foreign exchange, derivatives, commodities and pooled investments. Wholesale markets are covered in detail, as are commercial banking, investment banking, including capital markets, corporate governance, and the more esoteric areas of the City such as gold trading and Lloyd's of London.

The workings of the London Stock Exchange, including the electronic order book and SEAQ, come under scrutiny. The book looks at clearing and settlement, and at institutions such as the Bank of England, the London Stock Exchange and CREST. There is a lot on capital markets, and how London is welcoming foreign companies for listing. Media and PR come under critical focus.

The way forward

Reading is no substitute for investment experience, but can supplement it. It is no wonder that online investors build their own small library, and regularly keep an eye on new titles published. If today's module inspires you to follow suit, it will have achieved its objective.

Dynamic rules

- Read investment books to inform your practical investing experience, but not to replace it.
- Buy online and you can often receive a significant discount.

A final word

Congratulations on finishing this book. It is a sign of your real interest in online investing that you have got this far.

There is only one way forward now and that is through real online investing experience. You must open up a broking account, if you have not done so already, and start dealing in shares, putting the knowledge you have gained into practice.

Set aside some initial capital that you can afford to lose, take a deep breath and build – slowly and carefully – a real portfolio. Initially five shares with £1,000–£2,000 in each one would be a good starting point. But you do not have to buy them all at once. I recommend also that you get to grips with investing in shares before you try derivatives.

You can never find out enough about the companies and sectors in which you are invested, or are planning to invest. Keep reading and researching. Beyond this, the internet is the most bountiful source of ongoing global financial information and news available but, as we have seen, you need to be selective.

Soon you will find that you are part of a global community of investors. You can speak to others through internet chat rooms. Online, you can track your portfolio. Keep your confirmation notes and share certificates carefully. Also keep a note of any important conversations with your broker, complete with time and date. By checking how your investments have worked out, and the process you undertook, you may review how the methods described in this book are working for you.

From this book, you should have gained an essential grounding. *But it will only have truly succeeded in its mission when you have reached the stage when you can let the book go, kick away the crutches, and make your own investment decisions.* It is then that you will truly join the small band of successful online investors who do it our way.

Think of it like learning a foreign language. You may spend countless hours learning irregular verbs, head in your translations, ears glued to tapes. But the education is only a success when you have kicked away the books and tapes and can talk to the natives in their own country.

We are at the end of the course, but it is not all over. I would love to hear from you directly. Do get in touch, with comments, queries, or suggestions for improving this book in the next edition. Drop me a line via the publisher, or directly at info@flexinvest.co.uk. Alternatively, visit my website at www. flexinvest.co.uk. In the meantime, dear reader, I wish you an enjoyable and, above all, *lucrative* experience of online investing.

Appendix

Useful websites

The following websites have proved useful to online investors, and will be a useful starting point for your own researches.

Bonds

Debt Management Office (gilts)
www.dmo.gov.uk

Books

Amazon – cut-price books and online reviews.
www.amazon.co.uk

Global-investor.com – an excellent large online seller of investment books.
www.global-investor.com

Brokers (online) – stock market investing

Abbey Sharedealing
www.abbeysharedealing.com

Barclays Stockbrokers – largest stockbroker in UK – services include covered warrants, CFDs, will-writing, SIPPs and access to advisory service.
www.barclays-stockbrokers.co.uk

James Brearley & Sons
www.jbrearley.co.uk

Cave & Sons Limited – also CFDs.
www.caves.co.uk

Davy Stockbrokers – Ireland's leading stockbroker.
www.davy.ie

E*Trade – US-based stockbroker – includes covered warrants.
www.UK.etrade.com

Fastrade – no-frills service from stockbroker Charles Stanley, including fantasy portfolio service.
www.fastrade.co.uk

Goy Harris Cartright
www.ghcl.co.uk

Halifax – includes very low-cost share dealing service.
www.halifax.co.uk/sharedealing

Hargreaves Landsdown – also foreign exchange, CFDs and other products.
www.h-l.co.uk

Hoodless Brennan – low-cost share dealing.
www.hoodlessbrennan.com

iDealing – direct market access facility, CFDs and spread betting.
www.idealing.com

Interactive Brokers – options, futures, foreign exchange, exchange-trade funds, and bonds.
www.interactivebrokers.co.uk

INVESTeLINK – service of Walker, Crips, Weddle, Beck.
www.investelink.co.uk

Jarvis ShareDeal Active – a one-stop service for all investment needs.
www.sharedealactive.co.uk

LloydsTSB Sharedeal Direct
www.shareviewdealing.com

NatWest
www.natweststockbrokers.co.uk

Norwich & Peterborough
www.npss.co.uk

Redmayne Bentley
www.redmayne.co.uk

SAGA Share Direct – service aimed at people aged 50 or over. It includes covered warrants and investment funds.
www.saga.co.uk

Self Trade UK Ltd – 90-day stop and limit orders, free research and virtual portfolio, email price alerts, and CFDs.
www.selftrade.co.uk

The Share Centre
www.share.co.uk

American Express Investments – international service, and virtual portfolio facility.
www.sharepeople.co.uk

Squaregain – second largest retail broker in UK.
www.squaregain.co.uk

Stocktrade
www.stocktrade.co.uk

TD Waterhouse – includes two months' commission-free online trading, covered warrants and virtual portfolio facility.
www.twdtrader.co.uk

Teather & Greenwood
www.teathers.com

Virgin Money – go to UK section, then to savings, where you will find details of the Virgin trading service.
www.virginmoney.com

Brokers (online) – derivatives and foreign exchange

Berkeley Futures – futures, options, shares, CFDs, bullion, and foreign exchange.
www.bfl.co.uk

Blue Index – specializes in CFDs.
www.blueindex.co.uk

Cantor Index – spread betting.
www.cantorindexcfd.com

City Index – spread betting and CFDs. A trading simulator enables you to trade a theoretical £10,000 risk-free for practice.
www.cityindex.co.uk

CMC Markets – CFDs, spread betting and foreign exchange.
www.cmcmarkets.com

Finspreads – spread betting arm of IFX Markets.
www.finspreads.com

Forex.com – foreign exchange for retail traders. The service is owned by GAIN Capital.
www.forex.com

GNI Touch
www.gnitouch.com

Global Forex – real-time, commission-free foreign dealing. Free access to foreign exchange news, real-time charting and simulated trading.
www.globalforex.com

Halewood International Futures – indices, stocks, foreign exchange, commodities, and CFDs.
www.hifutures.com

IFX Markets – competitive foreign exchange price feeds directly from interbank market, CFDs and spread betting.
www.ifxmarkets.com

IG Markets – foreign exchange, CFDs, stock indices and more.
www.igforex.com (for spread betting visit IG Index at www.igindex.co.uk).

Kyte Group – long-established firm, servicing private clients in foreign exchange, equity options, CFDs, interest rate products, commodities and indices.
www.kytegroup.com

Lind-Waldock – a US firm.
www.lindwaldock.com

ManDirect – futures, options, CFDs, US stocks on margin, and foreign exchange.
www.mandirect.co.uk

MG Financial Group – foreign exchange for retail investors. The firm was established in 1992 and is based in New York.
www.forex-mg.com

Monument Securities – international derivatives. Chief economist is the respected Stephen Lewis.
www.monumentsecurities.com

ODL Securities – futures, options and warrants, CFDs, foreign exchange, gold and silver, mini-forex, and equities.
www.odlsecurities.com

Spreadex – spread betting.
www.speadexfinancials.com

Sucden – futures, options and foreign exchange.
www.sucden.co.uk

Covered warrants

General

London Stock Exchange – latest prices, training guide, morning bulletin and e-mail alerts, and analytical tools.
www.londonstockexchange.com/coveredwarrants

UKWarrants.info – independent information for warrants traders.
www.ukwarrants.info

Issuers

Dresdner Kleinwort Wasserstein
www.drkw.com

SG Warrants
www.warrants.com

Goldman Sachs
www.gs-warrants.co.uk

J.P. Morgan
www.jpmorganinvestor.com

Unicredit Banca Mobiliare
www.tradinglab.com

Complaints

Financial Ombudsman Service
www.financial-ombudsman.co.uk

Economy and foreign exchange

Bank of England – the site explains, among other things, the role of the Monetary Policy Committee in deciding on interest rates. Discussion papers and other data are available.
www.bankofengland.co.uk

Federal Reserve Bank of New York – about how foreign exchange markets work.
www.newyorkfed.org/education

Forex.com – about how foreign exchange works.
www.forex.com

National Statistics – the home of official UK statistics.
www.statistics.gov.uk

Exchanges and markets

APX Group – European provider of power and gas exchanges.
www.apxgroup.com

The Baltic Exchange – not an exchange but regulates shipbrokers and distributes data.
www.balticexchange.com

Chicago Board Options Exchange – US options exchange.
www.cboe.com

Euronext – the cross-border exchange.
www.euronext.com

Ice Futures – world's leading electronic exchange for energy trading.
www.theice.com

London Metal Exchange
www.lme.co.uk

London Stock Exchange – lots of valuable data, statistics, explanations and articles.
www.londonstockexchange.com

NASDAQ – the US high-tech market.
www.Nasdaq.com

NYSE Group – operates the New York stock Exchange and NYSE Arca.
www.nyse.com

Ofex – official OFEX website.
www.plusmarkets.com

Frequent trader platforms

Esignal – service that delivers real time data.
www.esignal.com

GNI Touch – Level II data provided for UK, US and European markets.
www.gnitouch.com

Interactive Investor – desktop trader platform.
www.iii.co.uk

Proquote – provides access to live market info, including Level II data, direct from the London Stock Exchange.
www.proquote.net

Funds

Citywire – covers retail funds and equities. The site ranks fund managers on individual track record, not fund performance. In 2001, Reuters bought a 25 per cent stake in the group. See under News, Research and Data.
www.citywire.co.uk

Morningstar.co.uk – comprehensive funds data.
www.morningstar.co.uk

Standard & Poor's – funds data.
www.funds-sp.com

Trustnet – free information about funds. Daily updated prices, performance tables and charts. A free portfolio management tool enables you to check your equity and cash holdings.
www.trustnet.com

International investing

JP Morgan's ADR website.
www.adr.com

Renaissance Capital – invaluable on Russian markets.
www.rencap.com

Investment courses/educational

Incademy investor education – gives free access to investing courses, written by financial journalists.
www.incademy.com

Investor's Business Daily – free course online (including technical analysis) from US guru William O'Neil. The site provides e-analysis, news and investor tools. Some services are subscriber-only.
www.investors.com

Proshare – part of the Institute of Financial Services (IFS), a provider of financial education.
www.ifsproshare.org

Securities & Investment Institute – the industry professional body. It provides online access to news, features and details of City courses and conferences.
www.securities-institute.org.uk

Sharecrazy.com – offbeat consumer financial website, co-founded by author and journalist Malcolm Stacey. It offers low-priced access to bulletin boards and other services, including an online tip sheet. A cartoon character, Joe Public, contributes to the site's charm.
www.sharecrazy.com

New issues

Financial News online – online sister service to the weekly newspaper *Financial News*. It informs professionals about Europe's investment banking, fund management and securities industries.
www.efinancialnews.com

issues direct – invites companies and sponsors to display details of new issues.
www.issuesdirect.com

The London Stock Exchange – publishes a new issues list, including all new companies that are seeking admission onto one of its markets or were recently admitted to trading.
www.londonstockexchange.com

News, research and data

Advfn – useful general consumer site. It provides news, data, views, and real-time prices on financial markets.
www.advfn.com

AFX News – real-time financial news coverage.
www.afxpress.com

AIMQuoted.com – news and discussions about AIM stocks.
www.aimquoted.com

AWD Moneyextra – an independent financial adviser. It provides impartial coverage of financial services activity.
www.moneyextra.com

Bloomberg News – timely and well-researched financial news and comment.
www.bloomberg.com

breakingviews – international financial commentary for subscribers. Set up by Hugo Dixon, a former head of the Lex column in the *Financial Times*.
www.breakingviews.com

Citywire – market news and data. See also under Funds.
www.citywire.co.uk

Compeer – specialist in benchmarking, competitor analysis and research services. It is worth keeping an eye on its main product, the Private Client Stockbroking and Fund Management Survey. The headline figures are reported in the press.
www.compeer.co.uk

Digitallook – The site offers news, analysis, personal finance, funds and free streaming real time price data and charts.
www.Digitallook.com

Economist.com – home to some of the sharpest minds in financial journalism.
www.economist.com

Financial Services Authority pension website
www.fsa.gov.uk/consumer/pensions

The Financial Times online – For a small annual charge, access to subscriber-level FT content, tools, personalized news alerts, analysis and a five-year archive. A higher level of subscription gives access to financial data for 18,000 companies worldwide.
www.ft.com

Forbes – US business magazine.
www.forbes.com

FTSE International – jointly owned by the *Financial Times* and the London Stock Exchange. It creates and manages indices and associated data.
www.ftse.com

Guardian Unlimited
www.guardian.co.uk

Hemscott – provider of business and financial data, as well as news and comment, directors' dealings, brokers' forecasts, mergers and acquisitions info and similar. Some services are free, and others are available on subscription.
www.hemscott.com

HM Revenue & Customs
www.hmrc.gov.uk/home.htm

Hoover's Online – delivers company, industry and market intelligence. It has a database of 14 million companies, and in-depth coverage of 42,000 global enterprises.
www.hoovers.com

The Independent
www.independent.co.uk

Interactive Investor – all aspects of consumer financial services for the consumer.
www.iii.co.uk

Investors Chronicle – leading share-tipping magazine.
www.investorschronicle.co.uk/public/home.html

Mergermarket – subscription-based service employing journalists across 43 locations.
www.mergermarket.com

MoneyAM – all-round consumer financial services site.
www.moneyam.com

The Motley Fool UK – influential all-round site.
www.fool.co.uk

Numa Financial Systems – useful links with derivatives sites.
www.numa.com

Onewaybet.com – informative on spread betting.
www.onewaybet.com

News review – summary of weekend City press, or filtering of articles related only to companies you want to follow.
www.news-review.co.uk

Unquoted.co.uk – bills itself as the home of the Off-exchange investment community. It has news about Ofex stocks, with an archive, discussion forum and links with Aimquoted.com (see separate entry).
www.unquoted.co.uk

Reuters – large international news agency.
www.reuters.co.uk

Red Herring – well-regarded US technology magazine.
www.redherring.com

ShareCast.com – news, and CFD mini-centre.
www.sharecast.com

The Telegraph
www.telegraph.co.uk

thisismoney.co.uk – news archives of *Daily Mail*, *Mail on Sunday* and *London Evening Standard*.
www.thisismoney.co.uk

Times Online – news and research data, including analysts' forecasts, statistics, ratios and charting.
www.timesonline.co.uk

World Gold Council – explains how to invest in gold, including derivatives.
www.gold.org

Zacks.com – brokers' reports and news (US site).
www.zacks.com

Penny shares

Biospace.com – biotechnology for investing in the sector.
www.biospace.com

City Equities – UK penny share dealer.
www.cityequities.com).

Pennystockinsider.com – a US guide to penny shares.
www.pennystockinsider.com).

Penny Stocks.net – advice on US pink sheets stocks.
www.penny-stocks.net.

Pink Sheets – long-established US-based provider of pricing and financial information for over-the-counter securities.
www.pinksheets.com

Recap.com – biotechnology.
www.recap.com

Post-trade services

CREST – settlement for UK equities and gilts.
www.crestco.co.uk

LCH.Clearnet Limited – clearing and counterparty services.
www.lchclearnet.com

Regulation, trade bodies and similar

Alternative Investment Management Association – global not-for-profit organization for hedge funds, managed futures and managed currency funds.
www.aima.org

Association of British Insurers – insurance-related explanations and developments.
www.abi.org.uk

Association of Investment Trust Companies – explanations and ongoing information about investment trusts.
www.aitc.co.uk

Association of Private Client Investment Managers and Stockbrokers – much of relevance to the private investor.
www.apcims.co.uk

Financial Ombudsman Service
www.financial-ombudsman.org.uk

Financial Services Authority – regulates the UK financial services industry – comprehensive and informative, with some consumer-friendly material.
www.fsa.gov.uk

Financial Services Compensation Scheme
www.fscs.org.uk

The Futures & Options Association – close to the market and has invaluable free material.
www.foa.co.uk

McWhortle – established by the Securities & Exchange Commission, the US federal agency which regulates financial markets. It is a warning about fraudulent web-based share issues.
www.mcwhortle.com

Serious Fraud Office
www.sfo.gov.uk

The United Kingdom Shareholders Association – this is an independent organization representing interests of UK private shareholders. Some outspoken comment.
www.uksa.org.uk

Spread Betters

Global Trader Europe Ltd
www.gt247.com

Man Spread Trading
www.manspreadtrading.com

Technical analysis

Australian Technical Analysts Association
www.ataa.com

Bollinger Bands – includes free tutorial.
www.bollingerbands.com

Building Wealth Through Shares – invaluable site of self-made Aussie trader and technical analyst Colin Nicholson.
www.bwts.com.au

Candecharts.com – site of candlesticks guru Steve Nison.
www.candlecharts.com

DecisionPoint.com – charting, some free, the rest for subscribers.
www.decisionpoint.com

Dorsey Wright Associates – best site on point-and-figure charting. Free course from online university.
www.dorseywright.com

Financial Services Institute of Australasia – includes the Securities Institute of Australia and the Australasian Institute of Banking and Finance. It offers a first-rate postgraduate technical analysis course by distance learning.
www.finsia.edu.au

The International Federation of Technical Analysts
www.ifta.org

Lit Wick – good on candlesticks.
www.litwick.com

Market Technicians Association – US technical analysis association.
www.mta.org

StockCharts.com – general site on charting. Chief technical analyst is John J Murphy, author of Technical Analysis of the Financial Markets (see Day 20).
www.stockcharts.com

Trader Tom – site of high-profile City Index strategist and trainer Tom Hougaard.
www.zanet.co.uk/tradertom

The UK Society of Technical Analysts – site contains useful explanations of technical analysis, details of courses and meetings, as well as free front page of newsletter.
www.sta-uk.org

Tip sheets and books

Eden Press – books connected with privacy and tax avoidance, private investigation, global entrepreneurial initiatives, buying degrees, and similar.
www.edenpress.com

International Harry Shultz Letter – lively investment newsletter which has attracted criticism about its recommendations but claims a loyal following.
www.hsletter.com

Growth Company Investor – newsletter with 12 dedicated researchers and journalists. It tracks over 2,000 companies and publishes 10 issues a year.
www.growthcompany.co.uk

McHattie Group – newsletters on warrants and investment trusts.
www.tipsheets.co.uk.

Michael Walters – website and share tipping service from the former deputy City editor of the *Daily Mail*.
www.michaelwalters.com

Red Hot Penny Shares and Fleet Street Letter – two heavily marketed tip sheets from Britain's largest publisher in the field.
www.fleetstreetpublications.co.uk

Techinvest – well-respected newsletter about high-tech stocks, edited by Conor McCarthy, who has worked for over 30 years in the electronics industry. Sample copy online.
www.techinvest.ie

T1ps.com – online tip sheet set up by Tom Winnifrith, a journalist who was the first editor of Red Hot Penny Shares. Strong on fundamental valuations. Shortly before this second edition went to press, the company acquired the four investment titles of Redsky Research. They include the AIM & Ofex Newsletter, the AIM & Ofex Deal Monitor, the Small Cap Shares Newsletter and Sizzling Shares.
www.t1ps.com

Trendwatch – tips based on trend analysis.
www.trend-watch.co.uk

Trading

Cybertrader – articles about trading.
www.cybertrader.com

Trading software packages

Sharescope – user-friendly investment software.
www.sharescope.co.uk

PrimeCharts – technical analysis software.
www.primecharts.com

Updata – technical and trading software company run by technical analyst
David Linton.
www.updata.co.uk

Index

NB: page numbers in *italic* indicate diagrams or charts

alternative investment market (AIM)   17–18, 19, 26, 38, 110–11, 112, 114, 116, 128
American depositary receipts (ADRs)   10, 162
analysts   7–8, 63, 65, 127
annual report and accounts   57–61
  balance sheet   59, *59–60*, 115
  cash flow statement   60–61, *61*
  income statement   58, *58–59*

Bank of England   71–72, 151, 163, 218
Monetary Policy Committee (MPC)   71–72
Barclays Stockbrokers   16, 25, 27, 29, 105, 213
Bloomberg (www.bloomberg.com)   20
Bolton, A (Fidelity Special Situations)   30, 59, 65, 77, 120, 121, 143
bonds   26, 47, 213
brokers   27, 41–42, 213, 216–17
bull market   6, 8, 129

capital asset pricing model (CAPM)   70
chart patterns   88–95 *see also* charts *and* technical analysis
  continuation   88–92, *89, 90, 91, 92, 93*
  reversal   93–95, *94, 95*
charts   76–83 *see also* technical analysis
  bar chart   79
  candlesticks   79–81, *80, 81*
  line chart   78, *79*
  point-and-figure chart   81–83, *82*
commodities   18, 47–48
  exchange-traded (ECTs)   48
complaints   48–50, 218

Consumer Price Index (CPI)   71, 72
contracts for difference (CFDs)   7, 16, 17, 26, 29, 172–73, 176 *see also* foreign exchange
  market/direct market access (DMA)   173
  trading   173, 176
covered warrants   26, 153–54, 217–18
  conventional warrants   153–54
  private investors' market   153

dealing online   36–40
  broadband/ISPs   36
  computers and upgrading   36
  dealing price   37
  online account   37
  orders   37
  trading systems   37–40 *see also* London Stock Exchange (LSE)
    market makers   38–39
    order book   38
    PLUS Service   39
    settlement   39–40
    trend   39
derivatives   26, 150–51, 207
direct market access (DMA)   29–30, 173
direct strategic access (DSA)   30
discounted cash flow analysis (DCF)   69–71, 112, 113
  alternative valuations using several models   71
  capital asset pricing model (CAPM)   70
  net operating cash flow (NOCF)   69–70
  qualitative factors   71
dividends   42

Dow Theory (Charles Dow) 77–78
dynamic rules (for)
  books and reading 210
  charts 83
  choosing an online broker 33
  contracts for difference/foreign
    exchange 178
  dealing online 40
  financial futures and spread betting 171
  financial statements 62
  fraud and dubious stockbrokers 195–96
  media and publicity power 188
  new issues 130–31
  online trading 11
  options and covered warrants 154
  penny shares/stocks 117
  pooled investments 123
  ratio analysis/macro-economic
    indicators 74–75
  share trading 144
  shareholders online 50–51
  technical analysis 97
  technical indicators 106
  using websites 20

Elliott Wave theory (R N Elliott/R
    Prechter) 96

fantasy/paper trading 32
Fibonacci theory (Leonardo Fibonacci) 96
Financial Ombudsman Service (FOS) 49,
    195
Financial Services Authority (FSA) 48–49,
    122, 151, 157, 166, 183, 184, 189, 194,
    226
  Compensation Scheme (www.fscs.org.
    uk) 50, 195, 226
financial statements 57–61
  accounting environment routine 57
  annual report and accounts 57–61 see also
    main entry
financial futures 18, 156–57, 162 see also
    spread betting
foreign exchange 18, 26, 176–77, 218
  as accessible market 176–77
  trading outlets 177
  training 177
fraud 189–95 see also stockbrokers
  Nigerian 419 191–92
  phishing 192
FTSE-100 index 7, 9, 31, 45, 119, 153, 162,
    166, 167, 169, 176

FTSE-250 38
FTSE International (www.ftse.com) 169

general depositary receipts (GDRs) 10
Generally Accepted Accounting Principles,
    UK (GAAP) 58

Hargreaves Lansdown 25, 29, 121, 214
Hemscott 18–20 see also websites for
    beginners

individual savings accounts (ISAs) 6, 26,
    27, 44–45
Interactive Investor 16–17, 18 see also
    websites for beginners
International Financial Reporting Standards
    (IFRS) 58
Investors Chronicle (www.investorschronicle.
    co.uk) 20, 63

Level I or II data 16, 18, 30
LIBOR (London Interbank Offered
    Rate) 160, 176
Livermore, J 17, 138, 139, 141, 142
London Stock Exchange (LSE): www.
    londonstockexchange.com 19, 20, 29,
    36–39, 42, 73, 109–10, 114, 115, 122,
    128, 153, 173, 182, 219
  and SEAQ 38–39
  order book/SETs/SETSmm 27, 30, 37,
    38–39, 153

macro-economic events 71–73
  inflation 71
  interest rates 72
  and key inflationary indictors 72–73
  and Monetary Policy Committee (MPC)
    71–72
market making/systems 37–38
markets 110–12, 128–29
  abroad 112
  emerging 10
  global 9
  grey 128, 163
media and publicity power 181–88
  company perspective 182–83
  internet bulletin boards 186
  press 182
  public relations 181
  tip sheets 183–86
  training and seminars 186–87
modern portfolio theory 46, 70

money management 8, 139–43
  buying 140–41
  capital commitment 139–40
  cutting losses/running profits 141–43
  selling 141
  unsuccessful trading 143
Motley Fool UK 14–16, 18, 32 *see also*
    websites for beginners

net operating cash flow (NOCF) 69–70
net present value (NPV) 69
new issues 32, 124–31, 221
  analysts 127
  big names 128
  book build 126
  clients 127
  demand creation 126
  grey market 128
  issue: flipping shares 129–30
  markets 128–29
  practical steps 129
  pre-marking 25
  press/media 127
  pricing 124
  secondary market 130
  syndicate 125
  syndicate desk 128
  valuations 125–26

Oldham, G 21, 25, 27, 29–30
online brokers, factors for choosing 21,
    24–33, 120 *see also* online broking, pros
    and cons
  and broker comparisons 32
  dealing costs 27
  and fantasy/paper trading 31
  image 26
  and limit orders and stop losses 31
  loyalty 32
  new equity issues 32
  price of trade 27, 29–30
  direct market access (DMA) 29–30
  range of services 26–27
  research and news: level I and II data 30
  smooth running and security 30–31
  trading hours 31
online broking, pros and cons 24–25
  accessibility 25
  fast dealing service 25
  low cost 24–25
  small size dealing 25
online trading 5–10
  and analysts 7–8

buying and selling, timing of 8–9
formative years of 5–6
history of 6–7
and investing abroad 9–10
investment techniques 8
options and covered warrants 145–55
    see also covered warrants *and* options
    analysis
  Calls and Puts 146, 147, 148–49, 150
  commodities options 147–48
  index options 147
  interest rate options 147
  intrinsic and time value 146–47
  options 18, 48, 145–48
  risk warnings and derivatives 150–51
  shapes and sizes 147
  strategies *see* options strategies
options analysis 151–52
  Black-Scholes model 152
  online learning/research 152
  strategy 151
options strategies 148–49
  bearish 149
  bullish 148–49
  butterflies and condors 150
  hedging 148
  speculation 148
  spider power 150
  straddle 149
  wheeling and dealing 149–50
over-the-counter (OTC) stocks/options 112,
    146

penny shares/stocks 109–17, 224–25
  buying and selling techniques 115–16
    dealers 116
    market maker tactics 115
    spreading risk 116
  cyclical 114
  growth and biotechnology
      companies 112–13
  markets 110–12
  recovery 113
  shell 113–14
  stock selection: management, and valuation
      and industry trends 115
  tax advantages 116–17 *see also* tax
pensions 26, 122
PLUS Markets Group 38, 39, 111
PLUS/PLUS-quoted stocks 111, 116, 128
pooled investment 118–23
  exchange-traded funds 122
  investment funds 118–19

actively managed fund   119–20
buying: fund supermarkets and online
        stockbrokers   121
multi-manager fund   120–21
tracker fund   119
unit trusts/OEICs   119
investment trusts/venture capital trusts
        (VCTs)   121–22
pensions/SIPPs   122

Random Walk theory   8
ratio analysis   8, 63–71 see also charts;
        financial statements; macro-economic
        indicators;
ratios; technical analysis and technical
        indicators
analysts/research reports   63, 65
discounted cash flow analysis (DCF)
        69–71 see also main entry
ratios   65–69
current and quick/acid test   68
and depreciation   67
dividend cover   67–68
earnings per share (EPS)   65
enterprise value/EBITDA   68
gearing   69
gross yield   67
price/earnings (P/E)   65–66, 69, 73, 112,
        140, 193
price/earnings growth (PEG)   66
price/net asset value (NAV)   66–67
price/research   113
price/sales (PSR)   69, 112
Put-Call   151
return on capital employed (ROCE)
        68–69
recommended reading (on)   197–210
City and financial news   209–10
derivatives and risk management   207
economics   201–02
fundamental investing   198–200
investment banking/capital markets
        208–09
technical analysis   202–04
trading   204–06
research/surveys   9, 21, 65
Retail Prices Index (RPI)   47, 72
retail service provider (RSP)   27, 29, 30
rights issues   42–43

Schultz, H (www.hsletter.com)   83, 104,
        141–42, 185–86, 227
scrip issues   43, 110

self-invested personal pensions (SIPPs)   6,
        122
Share Centre, The   21, 25, 26, 27, 29, 215
share trading   135–44 see also money
        management
categories of   137
limit orders, using   137–38
market position: trading base   136
and mistakes   138–39
professionalism in   139
risk   135–36
and screen-based news/data   143
and self-discipline and proportion   138
seminars   170
and trading capital, protecting   138
trading system   137
shareholders online   41–51
diversification   45–48
asset allocation   46
bonds   47
commodities   47–48
optimum size   45–46
holdings   41–43
dividends   42
rights issues   42–43
scrip issues   43
takeovers   43
investment clubs   48
regulation and complaints   48–50
consumer protection/grounds for
        complaint   48–49
Financial Ombudsman Service
        (FOS)   49
Financial Services Compensation
        Scheme   50
press/media   49–50
tax considerations   44–45 see also tax
shares/share certificates   27, 40 see also
        penny shares/stocks
and projected earnings   17
Slater, J   8, 15, 19, 66, 73, 109
specialist investments   107–31 see also
        new issues; penny shares and pooled
        investment
spread betting   7, 65, 157, 160–63, 166–67,
        169–70, 177
chances   169
closing position   166
costs   166
financial bookmaker, selecting   166–67
forward or cash bets   160–61
independent training   169–70
multiple exposures   162–63

risk, controlling   167
short position   161
specialist trading strategies   167, 169
speculators   166
Stock Exchange Alternative Trading Service (SEATS)   38
Stock Exchange Automated Quotation (SEAQ)   29
Stock Exchange Electronic Trading Service (SETS)   29
stock market(s)   18, 47
  online   5–11 *see also* online trading
  United Kingdom (UK)   7, 8
  United States of America (USA)   6, 9
stockbrokers 32, 189–96 *see also* websites, useful
  access to client lists   194
  authorized firms/dubious brokers 192–94
  regulatory warnings and legislation   195
  unauthorized firms   189–96
    boiler rooms   189–91
    financial services scams   191–92
stock-screening tool, Filter X   18
stocks   8, 17, 31, 112, 146, 162 *see also* penny shares/stocks

tax   44–45 *see also* individual savings accounts (ISAs)
  capital gains (CGT)   45, 116, 166
  Enterprise Investment Scheme   116
  inheritance (IHT)   45, 117
  relief on BCT   122
technical analysis   15, 76–78, 79, 80, 83, 84–97, 226–27 *see also* charts *and*

technical indicators
  chart patterns   88–95 *see also main entry*
  Dow Theory   77–78
  Elliott Wave theory   96
  Fibonacci theory (Leonardo Fibonacci)   96
  trends: using the charts   84–85,*85*, 87, *87*
technical indicators   98–106
  charting facilities, tips and training   105
  momentum: relative strength index (RSI) and stochastics   102–04, *103, 104*
  price   98–102
    envelopes   100–01, *101*
    MACD histogram   100
    moving average convergence divergence (MACD)   99–100, *100*
    moving averages   98–99, *99*
    stop and reverse points (SARs)   101–02, *102*
  volume: Accumulation/Distribution line   102–03
tip sheets, selection of   183–86, 227–28

value investing   8–9
venture capital trusts (VCTs)   121–22

websites, useful   10, 14–20, 29, 32, 46, 48, 63, 73, 81, 83, 96, 105, 111, 112, 116, 120, 213–29
websites for beginners   14–20
  ADVFN: www.advfn.com   17–18
  Hemscott: www.hemscott.com   18–20
  Interactive Investor: www.iii.co.uk 16–17
  Motley Fool UK: www.fool.co.uk   14–16

Index of advertisers

Barclays Stockbrokers   viii, xviii–xix
Cantor Index   v, 158–59
CMC Markets   x, 164–65
Global Trader Europe Ltd   xii, 174–75
Man Spread Trading   168

ODL Securities   xvi–xvii
Selftrade   xiv, 22–23
Stocktrade   vi, 12–13
The Share Centre   28, 34–35, 54–55, 64, 86